LIFE CHANGERS
(More Twice Born Men)
Narratives
of a Recent Movement
in the
Spirit of Personal Religion

BY
HAROLD BEGBIE

BULKINGTON BOOKS

"Madman! Look through my eyes if thou hast none of thine own."

This Book Belongs to:

SA
PIEN
TIA

SCI
EN
TIA

IN
TELLEC
TVS

FOR
TITV
DO

CON
SILI
VM

PI
E
TAS

TIMOR
DÑI

LIFE CHANGERS

(More Twice Born Men)
Narratives
of a Recent Movement
in the
Spirit of Personal Religion

BY

HAROLD BEGBIE

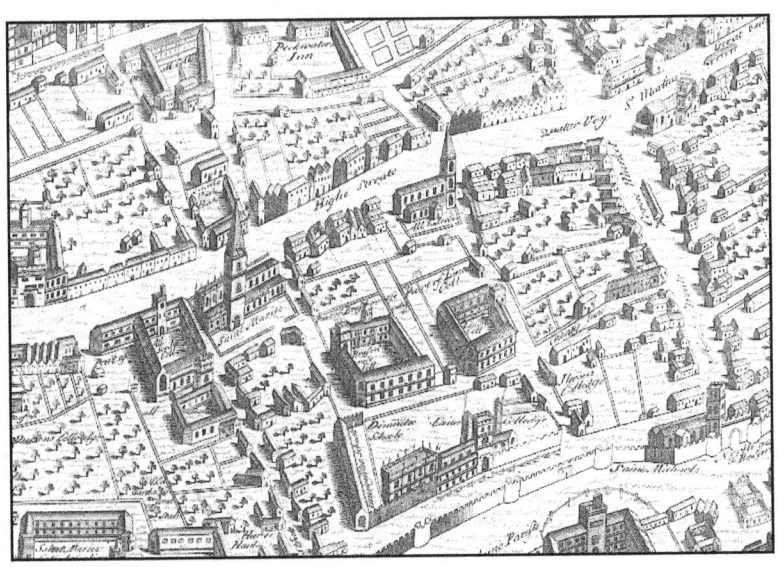

TABLE OF CONTENTS

Publisher's Note

Blessed beloved bookreader, you have found this volume in your vision. We hope you read on, but let us offer a few humble words. Of making many books there is no end, and a long preface is a chasing after wind. We pray you give us a moment's indulgence.

Our mission is to build a bridge into the past, before film, television, copyright, and internet swallowed up the world. Before 'content' was culture. If the reader finds friends from before the echo chamber, they may find armor and sword against the dreadful noise machine.

We are convinced that many authors and many books are ready to rise like Lazarus and reenter the world to remind the readers that their life has purpose; that their time should be valued; and their history is an honorable home.

This book was chosen because it shows that spiritual rebirth, and recovery from hopeless states of mind and body, have been occuring for a long time. The roots of revival are all the same. Unlike the last book by Begbie, set in the slums of London, this one chronicles his time interviewing the sensitive young men, the 'elite human capital,' of the Ivy League Universities and Oxford.

Despite the difference, the same spiritual malady requires the same sunlight of the spirit. We hope you enjoy.

Your Most Humble and Obedient Servant, (YMHOS)

Arthur Bulkington,

Melville Bay

Life Changers

New Edition

G.P.Putnam's Sons

XewYork & London

He 'Knickerbocker ^JCBM

1927

PUBLISHER'S FOREWORD

Life Changers is a sequel to Mr. Begbie's 1909 book *Twice Born Men*. That book, which we published, is about the Salvation Army doing work in the poorest neighborhoods of London. The Salvation Army of that time was a very different organization than it is today. Back then, the Salvationists held bible studies and revival meetings and helped criminals, drunkards, and fallen women renounce their wickedness, have a spiritual rebirth, and live in a new way.

This book focuses on the Oxford Group, which began in the Ivy League colleges of Princeton and Yale and then took root at the University of Oxford. It was founded and led by a man named Frank Buchman and was meant to be a revival of First Century Christianity. Harold Begbie describes this man and some of his methods, and several young men from the Ivy Leagues and Oxford, and what they found in the Oxford Group.

That might suffice for a few sympathetic Readers and justify this book. But for those on the fence, we wish to say a few more words on this. The three points we want to make, the duty of a foreword, are thus:

1) Why we liked it. Why it was worth our time to reformat, footnote, and republish.

2) Why it has relevance today.

3) Why it is worth your precious reading time.

We liked it because it's a postcard from a lost world. The elites of that world raised up young men who quoted poetry, fought in World War One, and felt compelled to become missionaries. Now we have elite colleges producing bankers and radical activists. The transatlantic Anglophone world that was beginning to take shape before and just after World War One has been completely destroyed. The British Empire is gone. The changes that have taken place since then have broken the link with the past. Getting a glimpse of this world is a good in itself.

We also liked it because it describes the process of spiritual regeneration, of being reborn, of recovering from a hopeless state of mind and body. This spiritual crisis, and the process of recovery, has always existed. While the 12 Steps are a clear-cut process for personal transformation, they are not the only one, and they did not come from thin air. We noted many similarities in the foot-notes. It is highly likely that the primary author of the Big Book, Bill Wilson, read this book.

We believe that there is an unhealthy split between the recov-ery movements and the Churches. One reason is simply that the recovery movement has forgotten its roots. Another reason is that the recovery movement has been pushed into ever more secular directions by a huge influx of state and private money that fund rehabs, treatment centers, and counseling services. This ends up infusing recovery circles with psychological terms and therapeutic concepts. This has arguably watered down the message, a point made by no less an authority as Joe and Charlie in their series of seminars on the Big Book.[1]

From the side of the churches, it is obvious that money, prop-erty, prestige, and politics, have put them in a difficult position. They have gotten involved in culture wars and virtue signaling, on all sides of the political spectrum. This make it hard for them to find a singleness of purpose.

We hope that resurrecting this chip of a book, and letting it find its Readers, will help rebuild the bridge between the two. Recovering the common history is a first step to this.

We also liked it because it brought us into some messy issues we didn't expect. Frank Buchman has some controversies tied to his name. These controversies require some comment.

---

1 We are aware that there are no 'authorities' in AA. But as a matter of common understanding, the Joe and Charlie tapes are a well-known and respected source and a good example of what 'Oldtimers' think. Another excellent discussion of this issue is "Gresham's Law and Alcoholics Anonymous," by Tom P., originally published in 1976. You could easily find more material on this, both within AA, and without.

He began his career as Lutheran minister in Pennsylvania. He had some success chairing a local YMCA branch at Penn State. He did missionary work in India, met a young Gandhi, then went to China. After this he started working at Hartford Theological Seminary in Connecticut. He formed student groups at the Ivy League colleges, Princeton and Yale. (Here he met Samuel Shoemaker, the Episcopal Priest who would befriend Bill Wilson later in the 1930s, when Shoemaker was hosting an Oxford Group meeting at his New York church.) Then Buchman went to England to do similar work in Oxford and Cambridge. This work was nicknamed the "Oxford Groups," and the name stuck. These Oxford Groups formed the prototype for the program of recovery that AA developed. Oxford Groups at New York and Cleveland helped the founders, Bill Wilson and Dr. Bob Smith, stay sober in the early days, and as places to bring newly sober alcoholics to begin their recovery.

The Oxford Group grew out of Frank Buchman's attempt to recreate first century Christianity. This has been attempted several times in the history of Christianity. John Wesley and the Quakers come to mind, but there are many others. The centuries of layers of dogma and disputation over theology blocks the core message. So people choose to sidestep all the traditions and lineages and go back to the first century practices as best they can. This tends to create new denominations of great zeal, but after a generation or two they get stale and bogged down in the same way. New and old wine and wineskins.

The Oxford Group did the same thing. They created new slogans and concepts. One formula is the "Four Absolutes," Absolute Honesty, Purity, Unselfishness, and Love, as ideals to strive for. These were standards one could use to measure one's behavior. Another part of the Oxford Group formula was the "5 C's" i.e. Confidence, Confession, Conviction, Conversion and Continuance. These were stages of spiritual growth. This was codified into the Six Steps of the Oxford Group: One, complete deflation, two, dependence on God, three, a moral inventory, four, confession, five, restitution, and six, continued work with others. These were the primary source of the Twelve Steps that Bill Wilson wrote.[2]

2 It's been said that he wrote the steps this way to 'close loopholes' that an alcoholic

Later in the 1930s, Frank Buchman rebranded his organization as "Moral Re-Armament." During the war many MRA members enlisted and fought. At wars end, the movement took on an anti-communist bent but also carried out a peacemaking agenda and multi-faith initiatives. Buchman died in 1961. The organization changed its name once more many years later, and it still exists today.

There are four controversies that come to light if you read about Mr. Buchman. We will note them here, and let the Readers decide for themselves.

The first two are interlinked. In brief, they are "it's a cult," and "he's a grifter." These are two big wormholes we cannot hope to address in a foreword. How one answers is going to depend much on one's general predisposition to religion, money, and success.

The cult accusation was made in the 1930s, in several books and newspaper articles. But if it was a religious cult, it is odd that it pivoted and rebranded as "Moral Rearmament," which was a nationalistic patriotic message aimed at church leaders and national leaders. Describing it as a cult of personality around Mr. Buchman might be a more precise description than a religious cult. But then you could describe it as Mr. Buchman's grift. Mr. Buchman's method, leading the Oxford Group and Moral Rearmament, was to target the wealthy upper class and recruit among the well-to-do. He was quite successful at this. He met many world leaders, and got lots of favorable coverage, and died a beloved figure. He and his organization became quite wealthy. This might be sufficient evidence for one to conclude he is a grifter. There are plenty of books on this topic, both for and against, both connected to criticism of AA and completely separate from AA.[3]

would use to try and wiggle out of doing the program in full. There are many books on Bill Wilson and the founding of the movement. AA History is now a subniche within American history and/or religious history. Ernest Kurtz was the first really mainstream academic to tackle this subject. Another gentleman named Dick B., from 'within' AA, wrote many books on the history of AA, and its roots in Christianity, the Bible, and the Oxford Groups.

3 *Saints Run Mad* by Marjorie Harrison, published in 1934, is clearly against Oxford Group. Herbert Henson, the Bishop of Durham at the time, gave a lecture on the Oxford Groups that is far more clinical and fairer, but offers some clear

But it should be noted that criticism of Mr. Buchman, nowadays, is either motivated by a general hostility towards religion, towards Christianity, or towards AA. We leave it to the Reader to make their own judgments.

The next controversy is about Mr. Buchman's remarks on Adolf Hitler. We will reproduce some of his remarks from a *Time* magazine article entitled "Religion: God Controlled Dictatorship," written on September 7, 1936:

> *"I thank heaven," exclaimed Grouper Buchman, "for a man like Adolf Hitler, who built a front-line of defense against the anti-Christ of Communism. My barber in London told me Hitler saved all Europe from Communism. That's how he felt. Of course, I don't condone everything the Nazis do. Anti-Semitism? Bad, naturally. I suppose Hitler sees a Karl Marx in every Jew.*
>
> *"But think what it would mean to the world if Hitler surrendered to God. Or Mussolini. Or any dictator. Through such a man God could control a nation overnight and solve every last, bewildering problem. . . . Spain has taught us what godless Communism will bring. Human problems aren't economic. They're moral, and they can't be solved by immoral measures. They could be solved within a God-controlled democracy, or perhaps I should say a theocracy, and they could be solved through a God-controlled Fascist dictatorship."*

These remarks caused trouble for Mr. Buchman at the time, and they *may* have been one more reason for the infant Alcoholics Anonymous movement to finally decide to sever themselves from the Oxford Groups meeting in Akron and New York, and begin holding their own meetings. Several reasons drove the early AA movement to spin off from the Oxford Groups. Catholic members

---

criticisms. You can also find newspaper articles from the 20's and 30's that are either hagiographic or ruthlessly critical.

For some writings that mention the Oxford Groups, if only to criticize AA, the works of Dr. Stanton Peele are worth looking at, as well as a book written by Charles Bufe, *Alcoholics Anonymous: Cult or Cure*. Additionally, one website called "The Orange Papers" is a compendium of criticism of the Oxford Group and AA on every possible topic.

were concerned about 'confession' outside the Church. Samuel Shoemaker says that one drunk threw his shoes through a stained glass window at an Oxford Group meeting. Joe and Charlie say that the alcoholics getting sober would smoke cigarettes and tell dirty jokes. There was increasing incompatibility between the Oxford Groupers and the newly sobered drunks.

We will note that Mr. Buchman's comments can be read in quite a negative light. But his sentiments were not out of place in the 1930s. He had the Russian Revolution and the then ongoing Spanish Civil War in his mind. It was a commonplace observation that fascism sprung up as a reaction to communism. Even a leftist like Leon Trotsky made this observation. Notable historians like Yuri Slezkine, who is Jewish, and the German historian, Ernst Nolte, wrote on the interconnection between anti-semitism and anti-communism during this time period. For our part, we affirm that genocide is bad, Hitler is bad, and antisemitism is bad. Beyond that, we have no opinion on Buchman's comments, except that it is useful to offer them as context for the Reader.

Now to the last and weirdest controversy. This is a harder task to face than the Hitler remarks.

If you read about Frank Buchman you will run across it often.[4] This book only addresses the topic indirectly with euphemism. We address it squarely, even if it is a bit impolite to put in a book's foreword. In several of the stories, the young men note a "secret shame" they have trouble with. They engage in physical exercise and cold showers. They use euphemisms, and talk around it, but they are probably discussing masturbation. Some related behaviors are likely to come to the Reader's mind as well. Especially if we consider the boarding school atmosphere of the individuals Begbie interviews. We might use the classic catch-all term, "lust."

When we read this book, we didn't expect this topic to come up as often as it did. We expected some stories more like Begbie's prior book, about down-and-out criminals or drunkards who recovered. But what we found were young men dealing with

---

4 See, for example, Glenn F. Chesnut's *Father Ralph Pfau and the Golden Books*, pg. 184-188. We recommend Glenn Chesnut's works to anyone interested in the pre-history and history of AA.

lust, and a crisis of confidence, and a crisis of making meaning out of the world. Their only toolkit was repression or 'discipline' or 'religion,' the 'stiff upper lip' attitude. So, in the interest of full disclosure, and to provide useful context for this, we have to give a few words to this topic. Our world today, and our attitudes, are so different than theirs, that we are trying to bridge a wide chasm.

Frank Buchman routinely confronted young men about their "sins," and often this turned into an interrogation about their sexual behavior, including their habits of masturbation. This happened often enough that it caused Mr. Buchman and his group to be banned from Princeton in 1923, though he and the group was later reinstated. Scoffing newspaper articles were written on this topic. We have to assume this is one reason why he pivoted from the Oxford Group message to the Moral Rearmament message in the 1930s.

What drove Frank Buchman to this, and compelled him to hone in on this problem, is besides our point. You can find some critics who have written on this and characterized it in a predictable way. If we let the critics have their say, it will still only give half the story. (That half of the story would presume that Frank Buchman was a closeted homosexual, or that he was sexually repressed, or religiously psychotic, otherwise disordered.)

The other half of the story is something our culture has lost altogether. The men in this story came from various walks of life, mostly upper class, but still varied widely in temperament, parents, upbringing, and outlook. And they all came to feel that the act of masturbation was something intrinsically shameful and sinful. It was bad in and of itself. Not necessarily because of religion, or authority, or cultural programming, or sex-negativity, or being a prude, but as a habitual compulsion that weakened their self-respect and confidence. It created enough inner torment and discomfort that they felt sincere emotional pain.

Their culture gave them no way of discussing any of this, or in talking about it freely. They had no tools to process this problem. Most of the men interviewed mention they had formal and distant relationships with their fathers. And it sounds like their fathers never gave them any advice or insight on this point. Suffering in silence about this problem probably worsened their behavior, as well as making them suspicious or cynical of religion.

So, when men are given permission to admit they have a problem, and are given a tool to let go of that problem, and this helps them recover their self-confidence, they will feel they have accomplished a miracle. When the solution to this problem comes from the deepest source of their culture, from Christianity, it resolves their inner conflict and helps them relate to the external world more effectively. They will want to share the glad tidings.

We don't want to speculate on Mr. Buchman's motives or defend his excesses. But if there were men who suffered from a sense of shame and guilt about compulsive behavior, and found a way to recover from it, and grow into more mature capable men, that is probably a good thing. That is what the 'take-away' should be. That is of use to those in recovery, and those in the Church.

Indeed, several 12 step fellowships that grew out of AA deal with problems of sex and love and intimacy. The two most directly related are SAA, Sex Addicts Anonymous, and SLAA, Sex and Love Addicts Anonymous. Even in AA you will hear people discuss some of their compulsive habits, in gross detail, especially if they used certain substances. This shouldn't shock people familiar with AA. And we hope it doesn't scare off good Churchfolk either.

Why is this relevant today? Well, it stands to reason that new technology, the internet and social media, have made many varieties of stimulating material available to almost everyone. This has probably increased compulsive behavior by orders of magnitude. This probably has an impact on the fertility rate. It has also empowered and enriched some objectionable corporate ventures. The internet has created many subcultures devoted to specific niches and constructed whole cloth identities based on habitual and compulsive consumption of certain content. The internet neologisms like "incel," "coomer," "gooner," and many more, suggest that the problem of masturbation has metastasized from a private personal shame to a worldwide social problem affecting marriage rates and fertility rates.

One more point that comes to mind on this issue. *Bronze Age Mindset*, a controversial book published a few years ago, talked about how "chimpanzees in state of nature don't masturbate." (Whether this is literally true in nature or not is beside the point. As a metaphor it unlocks a great insight.) This point is married to a larger exhortation about how many men feel trapped in society and need to find a way to reclaim their vitality.

We might connect these insights, and say that the secret shameful sin was at least some kind of coping mechanism for young men who felt they were not free, that the whole world was already 'settled space,' and they intuited they had no outlet for bold endeavor. It was a coping mechanism for an animal that felt trapped and powerless in a society that did not offer outlets for aggression, glory, conquest, the quintessentially masculine virtues.

A promising young man who goes off to Oxford or Princeton, without any honest fatherly advice, facing a boring scholarly and religious atmosphere, may feel trapped. This feeling of entrapment may come out in various ways. The young man has no one he can talk to about this, and a wall of silence is put up between his innermost self and what the world expects of him. Being expected to act a certain way, perform at a certain level, live up to an expectation, may feel like being an animal in a zoo. It is not a big leap to say that a drinking problem may grow out of the same feeling. Indeed, we might take a point from Chuck C's *New Pair of Glasses*, which says that the root problem is "conscious separation" from God, from society, from life on life's terms.[5]

The Big Book tries to sidestep these issues as much as possible, but it says, on page 69, "We remembered always that our sex powers were God-given and therefore good, neither to be used lightly or selfishly nor to be despised and loathed." And: "God alone can judge our sex situation." He brings the point home on page 134, "Alcohol is so sexually stimulating to some men that they have over-indulged." Let us read between the lines a little. A person

---

5 Chuck C. gave a series of talks later turned into a book, called *New Pair of Glasses*. It is not approved by the General Service Conference, but is a familiar part of the unofficial canon. We might add that his book makes some very obscure references, and is of interest to anyone who would be reading this.

may find themselves feeling deeply separated from society. They may pick up a compulsive behavior to soothe this pain. Compulsive behavior could be transferred from one coping mechanism to another. The Big Book gives a few examples. We might consider the example of the jay-walker, who cannot stop jaywalking despite risk of life and limb. Jay-walking may be a suitable metaphor for any self-destructive habit. Another example is Jim, who has "a nervous disposition," and who has ruined his career through binge-drinking. The common pattern is the "double life" a person leads, between their external appearance and reputation, and their innermost self.

The tension between the external role they play, and the innermost self leads to a great inner tension:

"The inconsistency is made worse by the things he does on his sprees. Coming to his senses, he is revolted at certain episodes he vaguely remembers. These memories are a nightmare. He trembles to think someone might have observed him. As fast as he can, he pushes these memories far inside himself. He hopes they will never see the light of day. He is under constant fear and tension—that makes for more drinking." (Page 73.)

When someone has fallen into an inner conflict like this, they cannot fix it by themselves. They need outside help, and often external help from psychologists or preachers or loved ones cannot make a difference. This inner conflict can be seen in compulsive gamblers, over-eaters, drug addicts, alcoholics, and in every type of compulsive behavior.

What's the point? The point is that compulsive, self-destructive, and addictive behavior can be treated with spiritual tools. We may not agree with how Mr. Buchman acted, or how far he went, but several men in this book give compelling testimony that he helped them recover from a personal shame that was bedeviling them. We hope that any potential Readers who have gotten this far are not put off. The AA member who finds this book and reads this far may want to consider that the basic recipe for spiritual growth, as outlined in the steps, can be applied to many other problems. The Christian churchgoing Reader who finds this book

Nor will that day dawn at a human nod
When, bursting through the network superpos'd
By selfish occupation—plot and plan
Lust, avarice, envy—liberated man,
All difference with his fellow man compos'd,
Shall be left standing face to face with God.
—MATTHEW ARNOLD.

may find it possible to apply their faith in a new way to solve personal problems.

We are faced with a culture that valorizes compulsive sexual activity even as birth rates fall. That culture is swift to silence anyone who tries to make moral judgments or objections. Any church or pastor who tried to address pornography or masturbation is made an object of ridicule. But it seems obvious that spiritual regeneration and rebirth would demand that men and women outgrow certain behaviors if they are to enjoy the life that God intends for them.

Likewise, sober members of a fellowship may feel stuck in some of the shallow cliches they hear all too often in meetings. Or they may want to deepen their understanding. Or they may have defects of character they cannot seem to dislodge. This book gives a new perspective.

We have been taken down some tangents in this foreword, more than we expected. We have gotten so far off the track that we have considered cutting most of this foreword and passing over the controversies. But, because we respect the Readership, we felt obliged to err on the side of disclosure.

It is clear that Bill Wilson read this book closely, and maybe more than once, since some of the lines are nearly identical. It's clear that on every topic besides drinking, he took the tack that "Good generalship may decide that the problem be attacked on the flank rather than risk a face-to-face combat." (Page 82.) He sidestepped some of these issues entirely though he left a few breadcrumbs one can follow to definite conclusions. The Reader may profit from these rambling tangents, and we hope it informs the volume that follows.

Preface

ALMOST in secret, a strange work has been going on for the last two or three years among the undergraduates of many universities, not only here in England but all over the world. This work, of which the general public knows nothing at all, and of which the religious authorities so far as I can gather have never heard, is the activity of a single person.

Something more than a year ago I made the acquaintance of this man, and learned from him that he considers privacy essential to his method, at any rate that he regards publicity as a grave danger. His genius, I think, lies in thinking with an intense preoccupation of individual persons. To him the man is much more than the multitude, the part infinitely greater than the whole, which is probably true in the spiritual sphere. Any idea of "mass production" in his work is to him dreadfully repellent. Therefore it is that he shuns publication of any kind, nurses the shadows of privacy, and never for one moment dreams of calculating his gains in statistics.

For a particular reason I was greatly interested in the work of this unusual teacher. I found that he was able to do, quite quietly, rationally, and unconventionally, a work among the educated and the refined which hitherto I had chiefly associated with a more exciting propaganda directed to the broken earthenware of our discordant civilisations. I discovered that he could change the very life of students and scholars in the course of conversation, change that life as profoundly and persuasively as ever I have known it changed by emotional missionaries among the ignorant and base. Further, I discovered that his method was distinguished by a single characteristic, which struck me at once as going to the very heart and soul of all religious difficulties.

We became friends; we corresponded with each other; at intervals we met and discussed the progress of his work. Then, in the summer of last year (1922), I accepted an invitation to meet a number of university men from both sides of the Atlantic who were to gather together in a house-party for the purpose of discussing spiritual experience and the best means of privately extending this remarkable work of personal religion.

Those memorable days began, so far as I was concerned, with disappointment, even with disapproval. I did not like the manner in which the early discussions were conducted; many of the phrases used in describing a really unique religious experience seemed to me secondhand and unconvincing; I could not help feeling that I was not merely wasting my time, but that I was foolishly permitting my nerves to be unprofitably irritated.

Some of the younger men consulted me in private as to my opinion of their teacher and his method of conducting these house-parties. I told them of my disappointment and disapproval. The first consequence of this confession on my part was a tendency to a cave; I found myself a rallying-point for discontent and mutiny. But this danger was averted by the extreme frankness and modesty of the remarkable man who had brought us together. He changed the manner of the public discussions, and left me more leisure to cultivate in private conversation a real acquaintance with my fellow-guests. From that moment every hour of my visit became interesting to a degree which truly one cannot well exaggerate.

The character of these men, some of them so brilliant in scholarship, others so splendid in athletics, and all of them, without one exception, so modest and so disturbingly honest, was responsible for my reawakened interest. They were men of the first class, men whom one may fairly call not only the fine flower of our English-speaking civilisation, but representative of the best hope we possess of weathering the storms of materialism which so palpably threaten to overwhelm the ship which carries the spiritual fortunes of humanity. It was impossible in their company to doubt any longer that the man who had changed their lives, and had made them also changers of other men's lives, was a person of very considerable importance. One regarded him with a new interest, a fresh reverence.

Yet—and this was perhaps the thought which most influenced me in those first moments of hesitation—some of these men spoke to me with troubled criticism of their teacher, disliking some of his pet phrases,[6] disapproving as vigorously as I did of his theological opinions, but all sticking to him with an unconquerable loyalty as the man who had worked a great miracle in their lives, and who was by far the most remarkable man of their experience in spite of everything that troubled either their taste or their judgment.

Among these men was a young officer who had not yet undergone a spiritual change, and who carried about with him, behind a charming social appearance, a soul that was haunted to the point of torture by a very horrible sin. I walked often with this man in the beautiful gardens surrounding the house, and he told me a number of extremely moving stories of his experiences, first as a pilot in the war, and afterwards as a trainer of pilots. He could not bear to think of the dead boys whom he had passed as fit to fly—many of them killed in their first or second flight. But every now and then he would turn from the war to speak of F.B.,[7] the teacher, expressing an anxious doubt as to whether even this miracle-worker could ever save him from an intolerable depression of the soul.

This doubt was uttered in no dismal or tragical manner, but with a smile very boyish and agreeable, and in a tone which rather suggested that he looked forward to his first private talk with F. B. as little more than a curious experience. He smoked many cigarettes in a rather feverish fashion as he spoke to me of "something on his mind," and I noticed that though the smile seldom left his face his hands trembled, while his eyes were seldom clear of the damp of secret tears.

On the last night of the house-party F.B. called this young soldier into his room just before ten o'clock. When the rest of us

6 "It starts to turn out that the vapider the AA cliché, the sharper the canines of the real truth it covers." *Infinite Jest,* p. 445.

7 We must presume this is Frank Buchman (1878-1961), founder of the Oxford Group. This name may be familiar to those who have studied a bit of AA history. But for those who haven't, a few words on his life and work and controversies can be found in the Publisher's foreword. The author, Mr. Begbie, is too polite to discuss such controversies. We mean no disrespect to him in having done so.

4

More Twice Born Men

went up to bed towards midnight he was still there. Next morning as I was entering the dining room I felt my arm touched from behind, and, turning about, found this man closing up to my side, his pale face and suffering eyes lighted by a strange smile of boyish gladness and triumphant serenity, in spite of all the marks of a sleepless night and great spiritual strain which showed behind the brightness of his face like so many bruises.

He asked me to go with him into the garden for a moment, and there he told me that he had been with F.B. till past two in the morning, that he had confessed everything, that (laughing quietly) a most extraordinary change had taken place inside him, that he was no longer oppressed, that he was indeed amazingly happy, and, best thing of all, he now had a definite work before him. F.B. said, he told me on a deeper note, that he must cross the sea to a far country, that he must there seek out a youth whom he had once put on the wrong road of life, that he must adopt that youth, bring him back to England, watch over him, and never leave him till his soul was right.

The profound happiness of this man, and his deep joy in the hard and difficult task which he had most gladly undertaken, made so great an impression upon me that I presently sought out F. B. and told him of my wish to write this book. I said that a book which faithfully described such wonderful work might do something to create in the minds of many people a new and intelligent interest in religion; that religion was losing ground and materialism was gaining ground chiefly because the power of religion to change the lives of men was now almost wholly unknown, or, if known, was regarded as an example of mere emotionalism working on weak intellects.

He agreed with this contention, stipulating only that no mention of his name should be made in the book; he left me free to conclude my own arrangements with those of my fellow-guests who seemed most likely to further the purpose in my mind.

In this manner the pages which follow came to be written.

CHAPTER I
ACCORDING TO THY FAITH

AT the outset I will make it quite plain how the method of F.B. chiefly differs, in my opinion, from the methods of most other men engaged in work of this nature.

But I must be frank with the reader, and tell him at once that F.B. would probably correct me at almost every point of my explanation, thrusting in with theological formulas which he himself considers essential to the success of his work.

I make bold to think, however, on the same ground which entitles the least of us to say that the onlooker sees most of the game, that I discern better than F.B. himself what makes his work so extraordinarily fruitful. This would be an insufferably vain assumption if I had not confirmed my opinion on several occasions in discourse with those whose lives have been so marvellously changed under the influence of F.B. They are my witnesses. In the third chapter of this book the reader will see how amply I am justified in proffering this particular excuse for what otherwise would certainly be an impertinent presumption.

When a man who has heard of F.B., or has met him in a fellow-undergraduate's room, goes to see F.B. in private, he usually begins by a statement of his theological difficulties.

F.B. hears him out. He never interrupts. He waits patiently and quite unemotionally, his eyes absorbed in studying the eyes of his visitor, until the young man's mind has emptied itself of all its intellectual objections to Christianity—those grave intellectual objections which distract so many minds, and which so few Christian apologists ever face with the uncompromising honesty taken for granted among men of science.

8

Then F.B. makes this remark! "It isn't any intellectual difficulty which is keeping you from God. It is sin." It may be anything, from the very worst and most deadly order of sinners to the victim of a bad habit reckoned by some people to be comparatively harmless.

In nine cases out of ten the diagnosis is true, for he is now so great a master in what he calls soul-surgery that he knows the facial indication of almost every sin which men think they can keep to themselves. But the correctness of the diagnosis is not the point. The point is that he brushes aside all the mental excuses of a distressed spirit and confronts it with the cold and deadly truth that it is sin, a sin which it refuses to give up, does not want to give up, and will not give up without a tremendous struggle, which is locking the door on its natural peace, its natural happiness, and its natural power.

The theory on which he works may be expressed in simple language after this manner:

Sin is a word which denotes a choosing. The will chooses the bad. It is its duty, in the interest of the world, to choose the good. It is fatal to its own peace and happiness to choose the bad. But it chooses the bad. This act of choosing constitutes the sin.

So long as it consents to the slavery of the bad it cannot perceive that to choose good is not only right, but a matter of the first importance to its own liberty. All sin is reaction; it is an attempt on the part of the human will to reverse the processes of growth—to go back, not to go forward; to descend, not to ascend. The will which chooses the bad, therefore, is in opposition to the will of the universe, that is to say, the Divine Will, the Will of God immanent in growth.

In order to be free from the tyranny of sin, and in order to gain the natural liberty of a will in harmony with the will of the universe, there must be, first and foremost, a *desire* for the good. Without that desire the will is powerless.[8] But let that desire exist,

---

8 Big Book (henceforth BB), pg. 59. Step One of AA: "We admitted we were powerless over alcohol -- that our lives had become unmanageable." Cf. pg. 45, "Lack of power, that was our dilemma."

however feebly or intermittently, and the enslaved will is neither helpless nor hopeless. Let that desire become the strongest and intensest longing of the heart, and not only can the will be delivered from its oppression, but a change of the will can be brought about so complete, so pervasive of the whole being, so creative in power and goodness, that it may truly be described as a new birth of the soul.

No man can sound the depths of his own natural peace, or rise to the heights of his own natural bliss, who is not conscious of the presence and the companionship of God.[9] This consciousness is natural to the soul whose will is in harmony with the will of God, but it is impossible to the soul whose will is not converted to the divine will. The work of religion is to create a longing for good in the soul of man, so that it may escape from the slavery of sins fatal to its own peace, and reach its highest usefulness to the purposes of development in a direct and living consciousness of God.

Consciousness of God, he holds, is the natural state of things. Sin is unnatural, and prevents the natural state of things from obtaining. Sin is unnatural in the sense that it is the will of the creature opposing itself to the will of the Creator. Always it is sin, and only it is sin, which blinds the eyes and hardens the heart of mankind. It may be the smallest of sins, one of those sins which we describe as merely amiable weaknesses; but let it be in charge of a soul and directing its course, let it be a sin which we find ourselves unable to give up, which we recognise as unworthy, and yet cling to, and we are living in the cold, we are moving in the shadows, and all our faculties are in gyves.[10]

I think this point of view helps one to understand how it is that many people who profess religious beliefs, and even devote themselves to religious work, are often so unattractive, so entirely lacking not only in power, but in charm.

It would seem that the whole matter turns upon a complete

---

9 BB pg. 51, "When many hundreds of people are able to say that the consciousness of the Presence of God is the most important fact of their lives, they present a powerful reason why one should have faith."

10 Gyves is an older word for "fetters or shackles." C.f. "Like a poor prisoner in his twisted gyves." Romeo and Juliet, Act 2, Scene 2.

unison of the two wills, the divine and the human. They must both want the same things to happen, they must both desire the same qualities, they must both be pursuing the same end.[11] Discordance between the will of the creature and the will of its Creator results in a weakening of the consciousness of God in the heart of the creature. Men may live very religiously and yet fail to dislodge their will from some form of selfishness which is fatal to their possession by the grace of God. They may be perfectly pure, and yet vain; or wonderfully generous with their time and money, yet intolerantly wedded to their own ideas; or they may lay down their lives for their religion, and yet never have loved anybody so well as themselves.

Perfectly to realise the divine companionship seems to depend solely and exclusively on one act of the will, an act which denies all the values of the animal senses, and embraces, not only with an absolute and unquestioning surrender, but with a profound love and an ardent craving for satisfaction, the will of its Creator. Hence at the very threshold of the spiritual life one is confronted by the challenge of love. No one can proceed far on that immortal journey who does not perfectly and most earnestly hunger and thirst after the divine excellence, who does not long for perfection, and who does not wish with all his heart to be rid of every selfishness which disfigures character and impoverishes spiritual power.[12]

It is a hard challenge, but there it is; and one must agree that the universe itself is hard. There is not much discernible softness in the laws of Nature. Spiritual laws are no less exacting, so far as one can see, than the laws which appear to govern the material universe.[13] Perhaps the attribution to the Deity of a softness, a vacillation, and a sentimentalism which would be contemptible in a man, has done far more to weaken in humanity the sense of the moral law than the earlier attribution to Him of such miserable

---

11 BB, pg. 85, "Every day is a day when we must carry the vision of God's will into all of our activities. 'How can I best serve Thee—Thy will (not mine) be done.' These are thoughts which must go with us constantly. We can exercise our will power along this line all we wish. It is the proper use of the will."
12 BB, pg. 62, "Selfishness—self-centeredness! That, we think, is the root of our troubles."
13 Cf. BB Chapter 4, "We Agnostics."

bad qualities as jealousy, vindictiveness, and a gross partiality.

Moreover, if we are quite honest and rational, must we not agree that this spiritual law is just? And if it is that, who shall bring a charge against it? History is the chronicle of an ascent on the part of man from unquestioning animalism to a disturbed moral consciousness.

Each step has been made by the deliberate choice of man between good and evil. No one has told him what is good. No hand has guided him from what is evil. First for his own safety, and afterwards out of loyalty to the past and desire for a nobler future, he has chosen good and rejected evil. Further, with each difficult ascent he has heightened the demands of good and widened the categories of evil. Each Alp of his toilsome ascent has revealed to him a greater height to be reached, a more difficult peak to be scaled. And the greatest of the sons of men, those who have carried the human race on their shoulders, have not complained that thus it should be.

Without this deliberate and unaided election for good it is difficult to perceive how any honourable progress could have been made in the life of the human race. And if our ancestors made that election, and if they opposed themselves to all the gross forces of materialism in the earliest and roughest ages of the human epic, are we now to complain, we whose lot has been rendered comparatively so easy by their heroic endurance, that it is a hard thing to expect us to choose good rather than evil, to give our wills to rightness and not to wrongness, to excellence and not to imperfection?[14]

The reader must bear in mind that we are not now thinking in any way of rewards and punishments. The idea of heaven and hell does not at present enter into our thoughts. We are discussing simply the question of individual human progress here upon earth. We are asking ourselves, "How can a man ascend from brutality to humanity, from weakness to power, from unrest to serenity?" The struggle is a hard one, as each man knows for himself, save only those whose souls are doped by the swill in the trough of animal-

14 BB, pg. 51. "Are not some of us just as biased and unreasonable about the realm of the spirit as were the ancients about the realm of the material?"

ism. In order to render that struggle intelligible, and therefore less difficult, we are endeavouring, in the spirit of men of science examining the physical laws of the material universe, to discover the spiritual laws of the universe of reality.[15]

In this inquiry we find from the history of mankind that ascent is the consequence of desire. The greatest of all human words, because it denotes the greatest of human powers, is the word love—a word which signifies desire at its highest intensity. What a man loves with all his will he finds it easy to obtain; the struggle entailed in getting what we want can be measured, and is absolutely determined, by the quality of our desire. There is no injustice in the condition, "According to thy faith be it done unto thee." That condition represents, indeed, man's idea of perfect fairness. To hunger and thirst after a virtue rightly commands that virtue; half-heartedly to wish for a virtue rightly brings only a fragment of that virtue into our possession. To obtain a living and creating consciousness of the divine companionship our wills must desire that blessing to the extremest intensity of love, certainly to the total exclusion of our own petty wishes.

M. Coué confirms the teaching of Dr. Milne Bramwell,[16] who told me nearly twenty years ago that auto-suggestion can do nothing without desire on the part of the patient. M. Coué tells me that his patients cure themselves by believing in the possibility of their cures, and that this belief is strong or weak according to their wish for healing. Many people afflicted with even painful diseases do not really desire to be cured of them—wherein we may see a spiritual parable. In any case, neither hypnotism nor auto-suggestion can give to the mind a notion which it does not possess; in each instance desire or tendency must be there, and all that hypnotism or auto-suggestion can do is stimulate that desire, to strengthen that tendency. "According to thy faith be it done unto thee."[17]

---

15 BB, pg. 10. "My intellectual heroes, the chemists, the astronomers, even the evolutionists, suggested vast laws and forces at work." Cf. also pg. 49.
16 John Milne Bramwell (1852-1925) was a Scottish surgeon, physician, and developed some notions on hypnotism and magnetism.
17 Matthew 9:29 KJV "Then touched he their eyes, saying, According to your faith be it unto you."

Christ enters into all these conversions. It is He who inspires the work. It is He who authorises the teaching. It is He who encourages the seeker to believe and the abandoned to hope.

In all this Christ is manifest. For not only is the teaching His teaching, but in Him as in no other being who has ever lifted up the face of man from the dust we behold the Will of God, the divine Will which has brought creation into existence and set in motion the laws of the spiritual universe. He impersonates for us the inconceivable, the unimaginable, the infinite. He humanizes the superhuman, He leads us so convincingly out of the delusions of the visible and so confidently into the realities of the invisible[18] that truly we can say of Him, He came from God.

No discipline could be more disastrous, I take leave to say, to the mind of a just man seeking to become a prophet of the Christian religion than a course of study in the average theological college of the present day. From such a gateway to the religious life most men of character turn back either with sorrow or disgust. Those who face the discipline learn that their preparation for the gospel of immortality consists in strangling their intellectual conscience, learning a few tricks of theological disputation, and harnessing their spiritual enthusiasms to the three-wheeled coach of ceremonial priestcraft. They find themselves ministers of Christ in a world which has no use for them or for Him—the Christ of their theology.

Surely there is a grandeur in the Christ of God which has escaped them. Surely, if they had penetrated His secret, they too would be life changers, they too would bring life and immortality to light. But these men, the overwhelming majority of them, the majority so fatal to religious vitality, have not sought to harmonise their wills with the Will of God, have not risen to the heights of spiritual desire, where the will of the creature finds itself in the Will of its Creator; rather have they laboured, with an intellectual dishonesty perilous to spiritual health, merely to out-talk with the worst notions of an inadequate theology the surest facts of material science. To be faithful to a tradition, to bolster up the ceremo-

---

18 BB, pg. 55, "We found the Great Reality deep down within us." Cf. 12&12 p. 98.

nies of a superstition as dead for all honest men as the Ptolemaic astronomy or the rites of Dionysus, this is to them the religious life, this the end and object of growth. "Many shall say to me in that day, Lord, Lord. . . ."[19]

We may see in such men as these, who commit, we must suppose, one of the most dreadful of sins in misrepresenting the love and justice of God and in obscuring the true purpose of Jesus, a confirmation of F.B.'s teaching that sin is a refusal of the will to conform itself to the Will of God. Science, criticism, philosophy, history, tell these men that they are wrong; they themselves are not only conscious of failure, but publicly confess and lament their discreditable impotence; yet nothing can persuade them that they are not the oracles of God. Obstinately do they stick to their opinions, stubbornly do they refuse to submit themselves to the Truth which alone can make them a power, to the Service which alone can set them free. Their position is precisely that of the traditionalist and the ceremonialist in the days of Jesus, and they cannot see it.[20] Their eyes are blinded and their hearts hardened. Never once have they realised that the crisis in spiritual life arises only when the mortal, hungering and thirsting after the things of immortality, empties himself of all intellectual conceits, all theological prejudices, and all moral egoisms, beseeching the Eternal Righteousness, with the whole heart and the whole will, for a communion which needs no rite and a companionship which is itself both a religion and a theology.

This, at all events, is the testimony of those who have been marvellously changed by conversion and themselves have become changers of human life. They all agree, whatever their various theological inheritance, that any form of wilfulness in the mind is a vital bar to a vital consciousness of God; that as soon as the mind, with real honesty and a consuming desire for that divine consciousness, hates its sin and turns to God,[21] the will is new

---

19 Matthew 7:22-23 KJV "Many will say to me in that day, Lord, Lord, have we not prophesied in thy name? and in thy name have cast out devils? and in thy name done many wonderful works?"
20 BB, pg. 48, "The practical individual of today is a stickler for facts and results."
21 BB, pg. 12 "It was only a matter of being willing to believe in a Power greater than myself. Nothing more was required. I saw that growth could start from that

born; and, finally, that henceforth life for them becomes trans-figured by a joy of which they had hitherto no conception, a joy which seems to consist of, first, a poignant conviction of the reality of God's response to their craving, second, an entire sense of freedom from a division in personality; and third, a sense of creative power in the lives of other men, making for a like happiness with their own.

Ruskin[22] used to say that he did not wonder at what men suffered, but at what they lost. The idea that immortality is something to be attained by the purified human will hungering and thirsting after the perfection of God helps one to realise the tremendous significance of Christ's question, "For what shall it profit a man if he shall gain the whole world, and lose his own soul?"[23]

Also it helps one, I think, to see a depth of meaning in that familiar phrase—too familiar perhaps—*The Peace of God.*

Therefore with what impatience, and with how despairing a regret, must those who long for the Peace of God see the Churches wasting their energies on matters which divide rather than unite, neglecting for teachings which obscure, depress, and after two thousand years of repetition make no difference to man or nation, the one great central teaching of their Master which saves the individual and glorifies the human race?

The future of civilisation, rising at this moment from the ruins of materialism, would seem to lie in an intelligent use by man of this ultimate source of spiritual Power. To make use of that Power it appears necessary that the human will must be sounding the same note, pursuing the same end, working in the same spirit. One of the simplest sayings of Jesus makes it clear that man's ability to draw upon this inexhaustible and immeasurable source of eternal life is determined by his desire for it: "Blessed are they which do

---

point." Cf. the rest of *Bill's Story.*

22 John Ruskin (1819-1900) was an author, poet, painter, and a thoughtful critic on architecture. The quote we think he is referring to is: "The highest reward for a person's toil is not what they get for it, but what they become by it."

23 Mark 8:36 KJV "For what shall it profit a man, if he shall gain the whole world, and lose his own soul?"

hunger and thirst after righteousness; for they shall be filled."[24]

With this understood, one can proceed to the narratives; but I would leave in the mind of the reader as a final word on the method of F.B. that the distinguishing characteristic of his work is the exclusive and pathological[25] emphasis he lays on the power of sin to rob a man's soul of its natural health—sin being understood, not merely as great vices, but as any motion in the will contrary to such excellence as that soul might reach by a genuine desire for spiritual growth.

This brief attempt to explain in untheological language the lines on which my friend works his miracles of conversion may help the reader, I hope, to enter with a quicker sympathy and a more rational understanding into the narratives which follow.

---

24 Matthew 5:6 KJV "Blessed *are* they which do hunger and thirst after righteousness: for they shall be filled."
25 BB, pg. xxxi, "He had but partially recovered from a gastric hemorrhage and seemed to be a case of pathological mental deterioration."

CHAPTER II

THE SOUL SURGEON

AS I have already hinted, the impressive thing in F.B. is that a man so unimpressive can work miracles—miracles which would seem to demand extraordinary qualities of mind. He helps one to believe that truth may yet be an even greater force in human affairs than personality.

In appearance he is a young-looking man of middle life, tall, upright, stoutish, clean-shaven, spectacled, with that mien of scrupulous, shampooed, and almost medical cleanness, or freshness, which is so characteristic of the hygienic American.

His carriage and his gestures are distinguished by an invariable alertness. He never droops, he never slouches. You find him in the small hours of the morning with the same quickness of eye and the same athletic erectness of body which seem to bring a breeze into the breakfast room. Few men so quiet and restrained exhale a spirit of such contagious well-being.

A slight American accent marks his speech, and is perhaps richly noticeable only when he makes use of American colloquialisms. The voice is low but vigorous, with a sincere ring of friendliness and good humour—the same friendliness and good-humour which are characteristic of his manners. He strikes one on a first meeting as a warm-hearted and very happy man, who can never know what it is to be either physically tired or mentally bored. I am tempted to think that if Mr. Pickwick[26] had given birth to a son, and that son had emigrated in boyhood to America, he would have been not unlike this amiable and friendly surgeon of souls.[27]

---

26 Samuel Pickwick was the eponymous main character of Dicken's 1836 novel, *The Pickwick Papers*.

27 "Soul surgery" was a phrase popularized by the group to describe their method. The book, *Soul Surgery: Some Thoughts on Incisive Personal Work* published by H.A. Walter in 1919, outlines the "Five C's" and went through numerous editions.

Fuller acquaintance with F.B. brings to one's mind the knowledge that in spite of his boyish cheerfulness he is of the house and lineage of all true mystics, from Plotinus to Tolstoy. His mysticism, indeed, might suggest even a surrender to superstition. He attributes, without question, to the Deity certain motions in himself which another might well assign to movements of his own unconsciousness. For example, it is his habit to wake[28] very early from sleep, and to devote an hour or more to complete silence of soul and body; in this silence he is listening for the voice from heaven, and the voice comes to him, and he receives his orders for the day—he is to write to one man, he is to call upon another, and so on. Psychologists would tell him that those orders proceed from his own unconsciousness, and are the fruit of sleep's mentation, the harvest of his yesterday's thoughts and solicitudes.

Such an explanation, of course, does not rob these motions of their spiritual value. But it is an explanation, I think, which may help those whose conception of the Deity entirely prevents them from believing either in His interposition or His colloquies with the human soul. It may help such as these to realise that a sincere acquiescence in the divine Will may enable the human will more perfectly to apprehend the spiritual influences of its environment, and to act more concordantly upon the intuitions of its own spirit.[29] Mystery remains; but it is a mystery which neither detracts from the unimaginable glory of God nor degrades the human spirit to the mechanical level of a gramophone.

The mysticism of F.B. shows itself more normally, and one might almost say more old-fashionedly, in his unquestioning conviction that there is a blessing in reading the Bible (quite apart from the literary blessing of feeding the mind on such beautiful English), and also in his faith that sincere prayer, even for material help, is constantly answered. But his great emphasis, I think, is laid on spiritual silence, and the article of his faith which more

---

28 BB, pg. 86-88 "On awakening let us think about the twenty-fours ahead. We consider our plans for the day. Before we begin, we ask God to direct our thinking...." In early AA this 'Quiet Time' was adopted and strongly affirmed by Dr. Bob and the Akron Group.
29 Big Book p.87, "Nevertheless, we find that our thinking will, as time passes, be more and more on the plane of inspiration. We come rely upon it."

than any other seems to give him his unique power is the mystical notion that in every man there is "a piece of divinity" hungering and thirsting for expression, a piece of divinity which best makes its presence felt to the soul in periods of silence.

He sees a significant parable in the scriptural incident of the blind man healed by the touch of Jesus.[30] At the first touch of those gentle fingers the blind saw men walking as trees; at the second he saw "every man clearly." F.B. tells those who come to him that so long as they see men in the mass, see them as a forest, their spiritual eyes are only half opened; to see them individually, man by man, and each man a piece of divinity, an heir of eternal life, requires the second touch of the spiritual hand—the miracle of conversion.

One of the phrases he never tires of hammering into the minds of those who desire to help the progress of men religiously is borrowed, I believe, from the Japanese: "It's no use throwing eye-medicine out of a two-storey window."[31] Drop by drop, and with the utmost precision, the extremest care, the medicine of God must be directed to the individual soul. He holds that little good is done by the extravagant methods of so many religious organisations to make Christians of men in the mass. He goes even further than this, with much experience to justify him, and teaches that numbers of those who are thus so heroically but vainly striving to Christianise the multitudes are themselves strangers to the central power and mystery of the Christian religion. Let me say at once that no small part of his busy life is devoted to the conversion of religious teachers, many of whom continue his fervent and grateful disciples.

How he came by this conviction of the personal character of religion, this intense conviction which drives him so earnestly and successfully on his happy way—for he is a man of extreme happiness—may appear in the following brief narrative of his life.

He was born in America, and at the age of twenty-four was ordained into the ministry of a Protestant Church. A theological

30 Mark 8:22-25.
31 二階から目薬 — Nikai kara megusuri. Applying "eye medicine from the second floor."

20

student at his seminary had accused him of ambition, and to correct any tendency in that course F.B. chose a most difficult quarter of New York for his initial labours. He was moderately successful in his work, but was conscious of an inner hindrance, a something in himself which prevented the great message of Christianity from "getting through." He spent a year as a missionary in the Near East, and in 1908 paid a visit to England with the express intention of attending the religious convention at Keswick. Here the miracle occurred which so altered his life that ever since he has been able to show a great host of people how they may obtain a like reconstruction.

Weary of himself, but not yet sick of asking what he was, and what he ought to be, this young American one day entered a little village church in Cumberland, under whose humble roof was gathered a congregation of seventeen people. The service was taken by a woman. "My feelings," F.B. has told me, "were very unhappy; I won't call them despairing; they were just feelings of great unhappiness. Grudges against certain religious people were there in my mind, fermenting; I felt that I could justly accuse those men of hard-heartedness, high-handedness, bigotry. They had always seemed to be opposing me—opposing my work. Yet the main cause of my disquiet was the knowledge of my own heart that it was guilty of three things, sticking there like glue, stopping all the free working of the generosity and happiness I longed to experience—selfishness, pride, ill-will. These three things were in my blood—selfishness, pride, ill-will;[32] I could not get rid of them; while they were there I knew that the better part of me couldn't function as it ought. Think of it—selfishness, pride, ill-will; and I called myself a Christian, tried to make other people Christians!"

The woman preacher—F. B. does not know her name—spoke

32 BB pg. 62-66, "Selfishness—self-centeredness! That, we think, is the root of our troubles. Driven by a hundred forms of fear, self-delusion, self-seeking, and self-pity, we step on the toes of our fellows and they retaliate." And "It is plain that a life which includes deep resentment leads only to futility and unhappiness. To the precise extent that we permit these, do we squander the hours that might have been worth while. But with the alcoholic, whose hope is the maintenance and growth of a spiritual experience, this business of resentment is infinitely grave. We found that it is fatal. For when harboring such feelings we shut ourselves off from the sunlight of the Spirit."

of some particular aspect of the cross—he does not now recall precisely what that aspect was, but he says that in some manner for which he cannot account her quite simple words "personalised the Cross," and that while he brooded on this idea in a reverie of mind there came to him, very palpably and with a most poignant realism, albeit with no suddenness, no dramatic intensity, a vision of the Crucified.

He was conscious at once of two shuddering realisations—the realisation of a great abyss between him and the suffering Christ, the realisation of an infinite sorrow in the face of his Master. These realisations dissipated the chaos in his mind. There was now no hesitancy, no feeling of a divided will, no sense of calculation and argument; a wave of strong emotion, rising up within him from the depths of his estranged spiritual life, seemed, as it were, to lift[33] his soul from its anchorage of selfishness and to bear it across that great sundering abyss to the foot of the Cross. There he made his surrender to the divine Will; there he lost all sense of oppression and helplessness. It was the work of a moment, and a gesture of his spirit invisible to human eyes.

I asked him to recall if he could the physical sensations of that moment of surrender, so that the reality of his experience might not fade from my mind, in the rather conventional language of revivalism. How would he describe to a doctor what happened to him? How would he tell that experience to a man who had never heard of Jesus?

He said, "I remember one sensation very distinctly; it was a vibrant feeling up and down the spine, as if a strong current of life had suddenly been poured into me. That followed on my surrender. No; it came at the same time. It was instantaneous."

What followed on this sensation of an electric current, he remembers, was the dazed feeling of "a great shaking up." He sat for

---

33 BB, pg. 14, "These were revolutionary and drastic proposals, but the moment I fully accepted them, the effect was electric. There was a sense of victory, followed by such a peace and serenity as I had never known. There was utter confidence. I felt lifted up, as though the great clean wind of a mountain top blew through and through. God comes to most men gradually, but His impact on me was sudden and profound.

some moments in a certain confusion of mind, not trembling in the body, but conscious of a long vibration in his soul, as though it was still throbbing under the shock of this new experience. There was no immediate feeling of lightness, no rejoicing sense of deliverance and liberation. He was conscious of a very mighty change[34] in himself, but for some time could only think of that change in terms of its physical effects.

He returned to the house at which he was staying, and told at the table of his hostess what had happened to him. He related this experience in simple language, and with no emotion, relating it, however, with the natural pleasure of one who has made an important discovery. There was a Cambridge man staying in the house, and after luncheon this man asked F. B. to go for a walk with him. They walked for some hours round the lake, and it was during this walk that both illumination and relief came to the surgeon of souls. He said, in his explanation to the other, that to keep his sense of the divine his heart must be empty of all sin, of every vestige of his discordant past. There and then he decided to write six letters to those men in America against whom he had long borne a justifiable grudge,[35] letters acknowledging his ill-will towards them, asking them for their forgiveness, and proffering his friendship.

The relief which came to him with this decision had a determining effect on his life; it taught him to believe that there can be no living and transforming sense of unity with the divine Will, no "God Consciousness"[36] as he calls it, so long as the heart is clogged and smothered by any obstinate trace of selfishness. There must be open confession, complete and unequivocating restitution.

---

34 BB, pg. 14, "For a moment I was alarmed, and called my friend, the doctor, to ask if I were still sane. He listened in wonder as I talked.
Finally he shook his head saying, "Something has happened to you I don't understand. But you had better hang on to it. Anything is better than the way you were." The good doctor now sees many men who have such experiences. He knows that they are real."
35 Steps 8 and 9 are making a list of those one has harmed and going to make amends to them. BB, pg. 65, "On our grudge list we set opposite each name our injuries."
36 BB, pg. 13, "I was to test my thinking by the new God-consciousness within."

The fact that he received no replies to his letters did not daunt the happiness which had now come to him from his unbroken sense of the divine companionship. That fact made him realise all the more sharply how hard it is—nay, but impossible—for a proud heart, however virtuous, to enter into the kingdom of love.[37] Moreover, his walk by the lakeside had brought illumination to another man, and now the way was clear before his feet. He had been changed; he could be the means of changing others.

The logic of this conversion can be expressed in very simple language, and in language which no man of science who has the smallest practical acquaintance with experimental psychology will feel it in his heart to resent.

A will which is divided, which is conscious of opposite tug-gings, which is never able to give itself freely either in the one direction or the other, obviously cannot function in the only way proper to a will. It is in a condition fatal to its health, fatal to its nature. Like a muscle seldom exercised, it is on the way to atrophy. One may indeed find it difficult to explain how a will which is not actuated by self-determination—a glad, rejoicing, and never challenged self-determination—can be thought of in any terms of volition, can be named a will.

A man who carries about with him such a will as this obvious-ly cannot be a happy man. In the sphere of the intellect he may make shift with unsettled opinions, and, like the famous bishop of Browning,[38] exercise his comfortable choice between a life of faith diversified by doubt and a life of doubt diversified by faith. But this will not do in the sphere of action—the true sphere of the will. A man cannot say to himself with any reasonable prospect of happiness, "I will live a life of love diversified by hate," or "I will devote some of my time to seeking truth, and some of it to propagating error." On the face of it, peace of mind demands a coherent will. The will must be doing what it wants to do—be it good or evil—if it is to be unconscious of hindrance.

---

37 BB, pg. 66, "For when harboring such feelings we shut ourselves off from the sunlight of the Spirit."
38 The poem by Robert Browning, "Bishop Blougram's Apology" about a faithless Bishop who dreams of being an "unbelieving pope."

It is plain to us that the distressed condition of F.B.'s mind was a consequence of his divided will. He half wanted to do a thing, and he half-wanted not to do that thing. Whether the vision in the little Cumberland church was subjective or objective, whether it was a genuine apparition—that is to say, an operation of spiritual law not yet investigated by the human mind—or a sudden obedience of the physical senses to a morbid pressure of nervous energy, does not seem to me of great importance. The fact which appears salient, and hopeful of intelligent understanding, is the fact that this suffering mind was immediately healed by a decision definitely and absolutely to exercise its will henceforth in one single direction.

There is here no argument for religion. A man half-afraid to go to the devil might find himself delivered from distress of mind by flinging aside his former hesitancies and entering with a whole heart and a whole will into the satanic service. The point is that all success demands the will at the back of it. A man cannot be happy in a life of vice so long as he is conscious of moral scruples; and a man cannot be happy in a life of virtue so long as any of his inclinations bear him towards vice. The demand of both God and Satan is identical—the whole heart.

The deepest thing in our nature, said William James,[39] is this dumb region of the heart in which we dwell alone with our will-ingnesses and unwillingnesses; "in these depths of personality the

39 This volume is a sequel to Begbie's title *Twice Born Men* (of which we republished an edition) and that title was in part inspired by William James *On The Varieties of Religious Experience*, a book referenced by Bill Wilson. The quote Begbie references is from an 1896 lecture James gave entitled *The Will to Believe*. From that source, paragraph 62:

As through the cracks and crannies of caverns those waters exude from the earth's bosom which then form the fountain-heads of springs, so in these crepuscular depths of personality the sources of all our outer deeds and decisions take their rise. Here is our deepest organ of communication with the nature of things; and compared with these concrete movements of our soul all abstract statements and scientific arguments—the veto, for example, which the strict positivist pronounces upon our faith—sound to us like mere chatterings of the teeth. For here possibilities, not finished facts, are the realities with which we have actively to deal; and to quote my friend William Salter, of the Philadelphia Ethical Society, "as the essence of courage is to stake one's life on a possibility, so the essence of faith is to believe that the possibility exists."

sources of all our outer deeds and decisions take their rise."

This is psychology—the psychology of world history, the psychology of every man's experience. We may hold this same clue in our hands as we go forward to consider the second stage in the conversion of F.B. He found that a great happiness came to him with the decision to exert his unified will in the service of One who proclaimed the reality of the spiritual world, and pronounced the values of instinctive materialism to be illusions. He discovered, in describing this experience to another man, that what had hindered him from long ago making this decision was sin. Sin is a theological term, but it is also a practical term—a term of world history, a term of every man's experience. It signifies error.

Sin is that which hinders the evolution of the human race and the growth of the individual man. It may be drunkenness or a false theory in art. It may be murder or pride; it may be dishonesty or intolerance. It is anything which impoverishes spiritual power, and deflects the personality from fulfilling its highest purposes. Perhaps it is best seen in its effect on a State. "What is the German suffering from," asked Professor Hobhouse[40] during the war, "but a great illusion that the State is something more than man, and that power is more than justice?" Sin brought the glory of Babylonia to the dust. Sin dug the grave of Athens. Sin destroyed so majestic a political experiment as the Roman Empire. Sin—the sin of unconscionable greed wedded to a piety that was either traditional or insincere where it was not actually hypocritical—corrupted the industrial achievements of England in the nineteenth century, and left us a heritage of social problems not yet solved. What sin has done, and is still doing, for Russia, Ireland, Greece, and Turkey, let every man judge for himself.

Another palpable aspect of sin is to be seen in those institutions of civilisation which law and charity erect either for the punishment or the curing of its victims. How many millions of money are spent in every chief country of the world on prisons and police-systems, on lunatic asylums and hospitals, and how

---

40 Leonard Trelawny Hobhouse (1864-1929) was an English sociologist and political scientist. He followed after John Stuart Mill. He was a liberal who disliked Marxism.

many men and women wasted in staffing them? Is not the philanthropy of mankind saddled with huge and increasing liabilities for the children of neglectful and even cruel parents? Are not the navies and armies of Europe, the expense of which presses so heavily on the industrial, political, and domestic life of nations, witnesses to a state of mind wholly at variance with an unbestial outlook? No man will argue either that sin is not responsible for by far the greater part of national expenditure, or that a State would not be in a better position to explore the future of mankind if it were not for its multitudes of sinners.[41] Is it not enough for us that we speak of a particularly contemptible sinner as a "degenerate"?

In the same fashion, sin operates disastrously in the individual. Its effect is represented by all those motions of his will towards things which offer no ultimate satisfaction to his nature. It stands in his life for hindrance and impediment. It is best described, perhaps, as mutiny towards evolution. The sinner is like a cell in the body which refuses to grow; it is the cancer of spiritual life. A man cannot do his duty towards the world who is not growing away from that world's past. The immense emphasis laid on sin by religion is justified by the interests of civilisation. The easy forgiveness of sin promised by some of the great Churches of the Christian religion is as perilous to those high interests of civilisation as the thousand enticements of a sensual materialism.

All this, I think, will be accepted by most men. The question remains, How are we to get rid of sin? How are we to free our wills from the fettering of the past? It is here that F.B. seems to help us. He says that the degree of our immunity from moral disease is governed absolutely by the degree of our desire for moral health. If we complain that we are slaves to sin, we confess that we desire sin. If we say that at certain times we are overtaken by sin, we proclaim that we are not travelling on the road of virtue. Sin is neither footpad nor assassin; it lives, and can only live, in the heart which does not love goodness with all its strength, with all its earnestness, and with all its appetency.

---

41 (Original author's note) The cost to Great Britain for the year ending March, 1921, of Law, Justice, Health Insurance, Poor Relief, Reformatories, Child Welfare, Inebriates, and Lunatics exceeded £80,000,000.

He came by this conviction in a manner calculated to make an ineffaceable impression on his mind. Soon after his conversion he devoted himself with great enthusiasm to the work of educating in the knowledge of personal religion theological students and other young men following in various ways the religious life. His idea was to help these eager and noble disciples of his Master to be more successful in their sacred work, to teach them how they should lay their main emphasis on personal religion, and how they should guard themselves against the destroying influences of ecclesiastical mechanism. But, at the very threshold of this new experience he encountered the old enemy. There, in the heart of even the theological student, he found this old enemy deeply entrenched, sin in one form or another holding the citadel against all the elegant deployments of divinity. In secret the theological student was fighting his sin—perhaps one of those secret sins which prey on spiritual vitality and attack so destructively the sensitive nerve of a man's self-respect; he was fighting it in various ways, orthodox ways, but fighting it in vain.

Then came enlightenment from F.B. That despised sin could not so tremendously afflict him if he loved goodness. Its strength was not great; the feebleness of the victim's desire for God alone enabled it to play the part of tyrant; it would disappear as if it had never been immediately he craved for righteousness with his whole heart, his whole spirit. Then followed a new understanding of the great teaching, "Blessed are the pure in heart, for they shall see God."[42]

One of the men who has been constantly in the society of F.B., who has gone with him on missions to many countries in the East as well as to most countries in Europe, spoke to me of the wonderful effect produced by this honest teaching.

"A man," he said, "who hides from the knowledge of the world a secret sin may go and confess it to a priest, but except for the mental relief of confession there is seldom great spiritual benefit; still more seldom is there a new birth. The reason is, as F.B. teaches us, that the sufferer is only *asked* if he repents of his sin; he is not subjected to a merciless cross-examination. At the moment of

---

42 Matthew 5:8 KJV.

his confession he does repent; he is there on his knees because he hates that sin, and wants to be free of it; therefore, quite truthfully, he replies to the question whether he repents of his sin with a pathetic affirmative and he is forgiven. Perhaps after the forgiveness there is a word or two on attending church services, saying his prayers, and reading certain books. But the man goes out from confession with the root of disease still in his heart.

"Now with F.B it is quite different. He would regard such a man as this with real hope. He often says that a person in pain can easily be healed; it is the person asleep who tries him hardest. He deals with the secret sinner not emotionally, not credally. He tells him that his sin is 'walling him in from God.' He exposes it as a deliberate structure of the man's will raised against consciousness of God. The man may protest that he desires this consciousness of God, prays for it, hungers for it, that his whole life is directed to acquiring it. F. tells him that he is deceiving himself. He says, 'God comes to us when we ask Him.' If the man again protests that he has asked God again and again to come to him, F. asks, 'With your whole will?' Then he explains that the sufferer is attempting to lie to himself, as well as to God, and that it is only disease, this secret sin, which could make him so foolish. From that he proceeds to getting the sin into the open, and showing it to its victim in all its horror and loathsomeness. He uses the knife, for he is a surgeon and no dispenser of drugs. He doesn't believe in narcotics; he believes in eradicating the disease, cutting it clean out by the roots.[43] He is terribly incisive, in love. He makes you hate your sin, almost yourself, but he makes you feel he cares for you all the time. After this it is a matter for the man's will. Hatred of his sin, and a real longing to be rid of it, a real longing for freedom and health accompanied by a passionate craving for the consciousness of God in his soul, sooner or later, very often immediately, will give him a new will. It is F.'s ruthless insistence on sin as an act of the will, a deliberate act, an act of the affections, which rouses men in this case to confront the truth of their condition.

---

43 BB, pg. 13, "I ruthlessly faced my sins and became willing to have my new-found Friend take them away, root and branch." Cf. Also BB, pg. 25, "Almost none of us liked the self-searching, the leveling of our pride, the confession of shortcomings which the process requires for its successful consummation."

"Finally, when he has done his work as a surgeon, he becomes a physician. He tells men whom he has thus awakened from sleep or delivered from disease that they may very easily, all the same, become spiritually liverish, and spiritually feeble, and spiritually rheumatic, unless they exercise their spiritual qualities. So he makes them, whatever their professions are or may be, helpers of other men, savers of other souls. In one way or another they have to be living unselfishly for the highest sake of other people. It is in that life, he tells them, they will find their greatest happiness, because it is only in such a life that man can enjoy an uninterrupted consciousness of God."

F.B. says that anything is sin which prevents him from being a miracle-worker. He teaches that it is necessary to hate sin, forsake sin, confess sin, and to make restitution. "This is taking a daily spiritual bath." The heart must be cleansed of all iniquity.

One whose life has been changed by him, and who is now changing others in a remarkable manner, describes the theory of F.B. in the following way: "There are two seas in Palestine, one in the north teeming with life—fish, fruit, crops, birds, flowers, life of all kinds. In the south is the Dead Sea—no fish, no fruit, no flowers, no houses, no life of any kind. What is the reason for the difference? The Sea of Galilee has a river flowing into it, and a river flowing out of it. The Dead Sea has the same river flowing into it, but none flowing out."

It is a good figure. Science and philosophy will not quarrel with it. A mind which receives and gives is a Sea of Galilee; a mind which receives, but gives nothing out, is a Dead Sea. It is a law of our nature that we enrich ourselves by sharing with others the accumulations of our activities, be they intellectual or material. The miser of wealth or knowledge punishes no man so heavily as himself.

The reader will perceive, then, that F. B. has common sense and the experience of the human race on the side of his method. He tells men that if they would be happy and undistracted they must be whole-hearted. His phrase "God Consciousness" may be translated into "apprehension of the truth," for the highest of which a man is capable is truth. His hours of silence, "listening to God," may be seen as meditation, when the mind listens to the voice of that higher nature which every normal man possesses in himself, and which is the driving force in evolution. Further, his teaching that we must hate whatever frustrates our growth, and crave with our entire will for those things which increase our powers, is a teaching which needs no religious sanction for the reasonableness of its demands.

Every man, therefore, may make trial of this method, whatever his religious opinions. Every man who desires to grow, every man who desires peace of heart and strength of mind, may test the truth of this method in his own life, without reference to any religion. But no man who thus genuinely endeavours to test this teaching will be able to doubt in the end that by discovering and proclaiming this law of man's spiritual nature Jesus, ipso facto, revealed himself as the incarnation of universal truth.

As a preface to these narratives I will conclude the present chapter with an explanation of F.B.'s work in the universities of the world.

Two Anglican bishops in the East, greatly struck by the extraordinary effect of F.B.'s personal revivalism among missionaries, asked him to pay a visit to their sons in Cambridge. They were anxious that these two boys should know F.B.'s idea of religion on the threshold of their manhood. That visit revealed to F.B. a very distressing state of things in the colleges of the University. He called a few of his followers to his side, and began a private work, to all intents and purposes a conversational work, among the undergraduates of Cambridge.

On his return to the United States he set a similar work in motion among the various American universities. Then, paying another visit to England, he brought back with him some of the American undergraduates who had become converted; and, returning once more to America, took with him English undergraduates who had undergone a like experience.

In this work he is engaged at the present moment, and he believes that a new knowledge of religion is spreading among men who may exercise a strong influence on English-speaking civilisation during the next fifty years. Some of these men more or less share his theological opinions; some are opposed to them; all, however, are agreed that he has changed their lives, and regard him with an affection which is one of many proofs I possess that his goodness has the true character of divinity—it is lovable.

> *Therefore to thee it was given*
> *Many to save with thyself;*
> *And at the end of thy day*
> *O faithful shepherd! to come,*
> *Bringing thy sheep in thy hand.*[44]

---

44 Matthew Arnold's poem, "Rugby Chapel."

CHAPTER III

GREATS

The writer of the following narrative is a man twenty-four years of age. He is regarded by many good judges as a scholar who may quite possibly make a valuable contribution to philosophy.

His narrative was written during a busy time in one of the German universities. It was chiefly intended as a note for my guidance. Its interest, however, seems to me so considerable that I have decided to publish it without interruption. The reader must bear in mind that the writer possesses in a very eminent manner the tentative and balancing mind of a "Greats" man. It will be necessary to make a certain allowance for his antipathetic attitude towards F.B. and also to read between the lines at those crucial moments in the narrative where feeling is vigorously suppressed, and reason, shrinking from a statement of the emotions, escapes from expression in a string of dots. The reader, I hope, will be able to imagine what those dots signify when he knows that this man has suffered very deeply, that through all his sufferings he has kept his courage, and that the most impressive quality of his courage is its unsparing honesty.

Let me say that one of the reasons which induces me to publish the narrative in its original form is the conviction that F.B. will not be able to read so courageous and appealing a statement without seeing that his influence is wholly independent of his theology. If one could set the spirit free from all man-invented forms, how soon might religion arise from its death-bed to save the world from the destructive delusions of materialism.

THE NARRATIVE

This is nothing more than a contribution towards investigating one particular phenomenon—the influence of F.B. And as the most striking feature of his work is that he addresses no monster meetings and writes no books himself, personal reminiscences are the only means available to estimate the aims and value of his work.

It will have been made clear already to the reader that F.B. is at least a remarkable personality, and as such possesses the gift of producing violent reactions in those with whom he comes into contact. There are few men among those who know him at all well who do not feel either an intense liking or an intense dislike for him; who are not by turns surprised, admiring, disappointed, enthusiastic, disgusted, afraid, or scornful of this apparently commonplace American. This is a very great hindrance to a fair estimate of him. I must, therefore, say at the outset that I write this as far as possible "in a cool hour," after living for nearly six months entirely out of the range of his influence and out of the sound of his name.

Perhaps a personality may be thought of as a piece of cord tossed from Norn to Norn,[45] as the old Germans imagined it. Life at least seems to be an interplay of elemental forces, which come to the fore one after another in the time-order, but must work ever with a material which is never quite formless.

If Wordsworth's[46] conviction—which is also mine—be correct, then not even the parents of a new-born child have a perfectly plastic soul before them to form as they will.

My father was the vicar of a small town in East Anglia— Cromwell's East Anglia, where the Protestant tradition lies still deep in the heart of the people. It was a Protestantism with all the rigidity of the Scots Protestantism, but without its democratic sympathies— a Protestantism of the *petit bourgeois*. It was impressed upon my youth that religion was a matter of wearing black clothes, playing no games, and reading only "Sunday" books on Sunday; of reading two "portions" of the Bible of the appointed length on week-days; of attending family prayers, which, one felt

---

45 The Norn or nornir, are from Norse mythology. They are three goddesses who weave the thread of fate.

46 William Wordsworth (1770-1850) was a prolific English poet. He seems to be alluding to his 1805 *Prelude*, Book 2: "My soul was unsubdued. A plastic power/ Abode with me."

instinctively, was principally for the benefit of the servants, who sat on three chairs in an exact row in the middle of the room. (It was for myself a severe Physical Exercise, and consisted of kneeling very straight up in front of a chair which I was not allowed to touch under pain of continual smacks from my mother. This was only relieved by the ever-present hope that something would go wrong, that my father would read the same prayers twice over or omit some essential part of the routine, which, indeed, often occurred, and was the signal for subdued giggling round the room.)

One can laugh now over much that one then cried about; but family anecdotes are not here in place; perhaps Samuel Butler's *The Way of all Flesh* would give the best impression of the religious environment of my boyhood.[47] And this religion did play a very considerable part in my life, and I took it as much a matter of course as being washed and dressed. I can only state as a fact that when I was first sent to school at the age of eight I knew an immense quantity of the Bible by heart, a knowledge which was useful in gaining me all the Divinity Prizes for which I ever competed. I had no inkling that my environment was in any way peculiar before I went to school; I had scarcely any playmate except my younger sister, and later, my brother. Did I reflect upon it at all? It is hard to say.

I will relate only two incidents, one told against me by my mother, the other which I remember very keenly as happening not later than my fifth year. My mother tells how, when three years old, after much admonition for some naughtiness or other I replied, "Though dark my path and sad my lot, I will be still and murmur not."[48] She adds that she has no idea where I could have heard the words. The other is the emotional recollection associated with a punishment by a particular nurserymaid. I had had read to me the Sermon on the Mount. I had a particular affection for

---

47 Samuel Butler (1835-1902) was an English novelist and critic. He wrote many books, including a translation of Homer, and advanced the theory that Homer was a woman.

48 From a Hymn written in 1834 by Charlotte Elliott, entitled "My God, my Father, while I stray," he is citing the second verse: "Tho' dark my path, and sad my lot,/Let me be still and murmur not,/Or breathe the prayer divinely taught,/'Thy will be done!'"

bacon fat, which was always a subject of dispute between my sister and me at breakfast. Ergo, thought I, I must give up my portion of bacon fat to her next day. The nurserymaid was unsympathetic, and my venture in unselfishness was treated as defiance of the powers that be. On the ground of other specific recollections I can say certainly that I was perplexed, first, how to square the treatment of the servants with my knowledge of the Bible—I think I always felt a certain sympathy with them, as also in the power of these other two beings who were on such intimate terms with God that they alone knew what He would punish and what He would reward—and, second, as to the wickedness of mentioning sexual matters. Until I went to school I was subject to no strong influence other than that of my parents (whom up to this date I hardly differentiated) and my uncles and aunts, of whom later.

My impression is that in the first stage "God" meant to me absolutely nothing but the power of my parents. I think it would not otherwise have been so easy to obliterate him on first going to school. I at once lost my sense of obligation to perform those prayers and Bible readings, and very soon I gave up the performance of them too. I do not connect the school chapel services with the slightest degree of religious sentiment. I had violent fluctuations of happiness and unhappiness, but did not connect them with religion in any way. When, at the age of ten, a serious-minded tutor tried to convert me, I laughed him into giving up the attempt. All that was silly; a sign of weakness. My ideal at that time, I remember, was the "wily Odysseus"; I made up my mind to accomplish in the school through diplomacy what seemed through lack of athletic prowess impossible. To some extent I succeeded. I thought: "One day I shall be able to manage my father too."

In this temper of cynical Positivism I was probably a very unamiable person when, at thirteen, I left my private school for one of the big public schools. I was deservedly, if somewhat severely, repressed in my first two years there, and distaste for my home grew with my un-happiness at school. I could no longer play with my sister, and I had found no other interests there. I was rather forcibly driven in upon myself. My antipathy to my parents grew and grew during these two years, till it assumed the proportions of a black cloud over my life, and was invested with the characteristics of all the tyrants and monsters who were ready to hand in the history lessons, and particularly in the Greek history. I remember a letter to my father at about my fourteenth year in which I held ardently in the spirit of Herodotus or Sophocles on the necessity of obeying my tutor as officer of the school to which I belonged, and the necessity of disobeying him as mere instrument of autocratic parents. I attributed every misfortune which befell me at school to the secret machinations of my parents with the authorities. The God of my childhood had gradually become my Devil.[49]

At this stage the conflict had certainly no strictly religious significance. From the religious point of view, perhaps, the only event of note was the growing influence in my fourteenth and fifteenth years of a somewhat older boy, who introduced me to the mysteries of Anglo-Catholicism. He was a personality likely to attract; diversely brilliant, subtle, humorous, combining with these intellectual gifts a sympathy which later degenerated into softness. His influence was very transitory, but I learned from him two things which were not so unconnected as they appear. First he really reawoke my belief in the possibility of a real personal religion, which, in spite of its elaborate appeal to my intellectual snobbishness, was far more real and vital than anything I had experienced before. From that moment religion became a factor in my life, curious as were the phases that it underwent. Second, he taught me to admire Swinburne.[50]

Curiously enough, I soon after came up against real religion in the other camp, through a visit to an extremely pious Protestant lady who tried to persuade me, by means of the book of Revelation and an equation of the Beast with the Roman Catholic Church, that the world would come to an end in 1915. I was really upset by this point of view, and prayed continually for a miracle to decide which of the two extremes was favoured by God. But this Protestantism had no chance, with its superficial relationship

---

49 BB, pg. 11, "Judging from what I had seen in Europe and since, the power of God in human affairs was negligible, the Brotherhood of Man a grim jest. If there was a Devil, he seemed the Boss Universal, and he certainly had me."
50 Algernon Charles Swinburne (1837-1909) was an English poet and playwright and critic. He had an interesting personal life. He was nominated for the Nobel Prize for many years but never won. T.S. Eliot admired him.

to the religion of my home. I stealthily read Catholic books, and gloried in the possession of a God in whom my parents had no part nor lot. I was immensely happier now. Under the spell of it I was confirmed.

This development lasted, if I remember rightly, about eighteen months. Together with concurrent "good fortune"? of various sorts it had an effect on my life. I found in the Communion Service more than I had believed possible. In the end it broke inevitably on the one hidden rock of insincerity. I had the first open outburst of violence against my parents shortly before my confirmation, in which I let off the suppressed emotions of years. I was repressed after that more than ever, and humiliated before my greatest friends; in return I comforted myself with the Imprecatory Psalms.

About eighteen months after my confirmation matters came to a crisis in this direction. From seventeen till twenty-two I was occupied above all things in a long and bitter struggle against my parents.... Starting with a quarrel about money, it involved eventually my sister and brother, most of my relatives, and most of my teachers. There were periods of superficial calm, but I think the feeling of tension and the desire to avoid each other was at no time absent during that period, and the fact of the struggle had a very great effect on my internal development.

I feel still that there was something elemental and necessary about the struggle. It was a fight for a bare minimum of freedom, which had to come sooner or later, but it was embittered by the religious problems involved. It was easy enough to form the idea that my father was acting dishonestly; easy also to believe that he was ill-treating my sister and trying to separate her from me. To all such reproaches my father had one method of reply —a deluge of lectures, sermons, pamphlets, threatening the wrath of God upon anyone who ventured to question anything that their parents said or did. This was accompanied by more practical threats through the medium of my house master, and eventually the head master. I got from them much real but timid sympathy, as I thought it; I got from another official of the school not only the degree of independence which I needed to avoid my home in the holidays, and to avoid having to ask for pocket money, but also a lasting friendship which had a great effect upon my life.

But at first I had no such older friend to lean upon. I played eagerly my father's own game; I countered his texts with other texts; I felt a certain Schadenfreude in this diplomatic game of trying to put the other party in the wrong. Only it was no game then, but terrible earnest; I felt myself a Crusader, not only for my freedom, but for my God, for the protection of the Oppressed (my younger brother and sisters), for Liberty of Belief. Perhaps I lived again the history of my people of East Anglia. I did believe passionately in a God who was compatible with reason and liberty of thought, and when I expressed these sentiments, I was told that I must be kept from contaminating my family with such dangerous ideas. I was denounced on all occasions as an Atheist and Socialist. I had then no notion of the economic significance of Socialism; I was under the influence of Bernard Shaw and William Morris[51], but still more of Tolstoy. As a prefect and as a cadet officer I tried to put my Tolstoyian principles into effect, with rather mixed success. As is usual with youth, I painted everything in vivid whites and blacks. As secretary of a debating club I undertook a campaign against corrupt elections. I refused to make use of my privilege of "fagging" the smaller boys.[52] I practised asceticisms, such as having no fire in my room for a whole winter, or sitting up and meditating all night. But perhaps that belongs to a later stage.

I said to myself one day, "What if I am an Atheist? What if my father represents, not a misstatement of Christianity, but Christianity in itself and in its essence? All the tyrants and obscurantists since the world began have based their claims on Divine Right, on a Divine Revelation where there is no room for reason. All the religious wars which have devastated the earth have sprung from this essence of Christianity as a Revealed Religion. It can have no place in a world of democracy and enlightenment."

My hero was no longer Tolstoy; Shelley and Swinburne in-

---

51 William Morris (1843-1892) was an English textile designer, writer, artist, and a socialist of the 'utopian' variety.

52 In British boarding school, younger pupils were required to act as personal servants of the older students. This was called "fagging," and would be a mix of verbal, physical, and sometimes sexual abuse. British boarding schools are infamous for their subterranean climate of homosexuality and pederasty.

spired my hopeful moods, and Marcus Aurelius and the Buddha my depressions. The last I owed to a very gifted boy whom I knew at that time, for me one of the great losses of the war. I threw myself into my new mission, which was nothing less than the destruction of Christianity.

I called myself a Pantheist, and the sense of the unseen remained strong with me. But I never missed an opportunity of diverting an essay or a speech into a polemic against Christianity. I devoted much ingenuity to making out St. Paul to be a Pantheist; I spent hours of argument upon the head master; with the greatest difficulty I obtained permission to recite Swinburne's "Hymn to Man" to the assembled school; and finally I deluged my father with blasphemies, spoken, written, and printed. Perhaps this was the motive of the whole; I think it does not explain everything.

Out of the many personalities who left their mark upon my school life, of whom I make no mention, I must except the new head master, who came on the scene during my last terms. He was a man whom I admired at once for his intellect, and came gradually to love for the greatness of soul concealed under a somewhat capricious humour. He was the first person who was neither shocked nor contemptuous over my anti-Christian crusade; he made me feel that he was personally sorry, and that I was missing the greatest thing in the world. He infected me with his own enthusiasm for his own heroes, St. Paul, St. Francis, Amos, Browning. He was a hero-worshipper. He also had in a very high degree the sense of God in nature and in history which had always been with me to some extent, only, on account of his personal Christianity, it was in him a living, moving force. He gave me the impulse to worship; he convinced me that for a keen and candid mind Christianity was compatible with liberty. He is not understood, perhaps through his own fault; he produced a very unfavourable impression upon F.B. He did not make Christianity practical in my life, but he was a very great inspiration for the coming years.

My years in the army, from the religious point of view, were blank and meagre. My longed-for financial independence improved my relationship with my parents for a few months, until a much more serious cause of trouble arose. I conceived that they were trying by baseless slanders to cut me off from all my friends and to bring me into trouble with my regimental authorities. I did what I knew would most hurt my mother's affection and my father's pride; I refused to see them before being sent to France.

The reply was a storm of denunciatory tracts, which followed me everywhere around France and Germany, letters rejoicing at the judgment of God when I failed in an examination, letters announcing my father's determination to prevent me getting a job or going to the University until I proved more tractable and apologised for my conduct. The atmosphere of a fashionable regiment was not favourable. I hardened and embittered my heart, and set myself to win a materially full life, if the stars in their courses fought against me.

In this spirit I went to Oxford, almost without money or hope of having enough to live upon. And yet my belief in God was never quite dead. Three things kept it alive—a change of station to the Yorkshire moors, my first taste of the hills, with all that that means; a couple of months lived among some very unfortunate people, which made me conscious of my longing and of my ineffectiveness to help; and, most of all, an act of absolutely unexpected Christian generosity, which enabled me to live at Oxford and reawoke my sense of the undeserved goodness of God to me. For the second time in my life, He saved me through the intervention of an absolute stranger from a belief that selfish materialism is the only active force among mankind.

My University years were years of rebuilding. The systematic study of philosophy and of remote history, into which I plunged passionately, had an overwhelming effect. It took the edge off my harsh dogmatisms. I attacked Christianity, as before, at every opportunity in debate and private argument, but in a different spirit. I began to wish it might be true. I preached Socialism as the truth of Christianity. I could not help being impressed by the college chaplain and by the "Religion and Life" group in Oxford, who seemed to have a real religion which was compatible with freedom and honesty of thought. But above all I was impressed by two undergraduate friends, temperamentally very different from each other and from myself, in no way remarkable in the college except as being real Christians.

One of them, M., was a man considerably older than myself, who, after a career in the Civil Service, had decided to give up his prospects there and become ordained in the English Church. He had no particular intellect, and I own with shame to having felt sometimes embarrassed by his company, but he had a great heart. He used to treat me like a father, sharing all my depressions and irritations. He used to flatter my vanity by asking my opinion "as a philosopher" upon theological questions; and when I railed against the Church he would answer me as far as he could and when he could not, then he would beam all over and say softly to himself, "Dear creature!" I came to know gradually of his influence in other quarters of the college; he felt a mission to "heal those who are broken in heart." He had a mystical and contemplative tempera-ment, which was quite compatible with a taste for giving riotous dinner-parties.

My other friend, J., was peculiarly unlike him in most respects. A person of abundant energy, he used to butt about the world, breaking his head against all the walls of unreason and unrigh-teousness he could find. He was absolutely fearless, and participat-ed in every mad rag which undergraduate ingenuity could devise. He used to campaign furiously against every abuse in the college and in favour of all the "depressed classes" of the University—the workmen of Ruskin College, the scouts, the women, and the Indians. He had little theoretical but much practical interest in discussion; he had a pathetic belief in the possibility of convincing people by reason, and used to spend his time bringing incompat-ible people together at meals for their mutual education. He had a great gift of winning the confidence of absolute strangers, such as Japs and peasant women. He was absolutely irrepressible and indepressible.

I had the privilege of travelling with him a good deal in the country. I learned there what the keeping in touch with God through prayer meant to him. I envied him his strength and I envied his absolute thoughtlessness for himself. Many were our discussions, lasting far into the night, round a fire, curled up in the arm-chairs which only Oxford understands, or lying in a canoe under the moonlight and the willows of the Hinksey stream.

We would talk with that sense of leisure and delight in pure argument for its own sake that one only has during one's first year at the University, when one has not yet learned to shrink before the great unsolved questions of the world. We were both reading philosophy. I was thoroughly under the spell of Hegel (not the subjective nihilists who claim to be his followers in England, but the master himself) and of Plato, whom I rediscovered through the great German idealists. I think I clung to this belief in the progress of Reason through the world, not because I could see her traces, but just because I could not see them. Where others went easily by instinct, I felt I had to beat out a way painfully through the jungle of things. My earth was so formless and void it must conceal somewhere the form-giving Spirit. Life could not be just this that I experienced. I could not rid myself of the persuasion that St. Paul formulated, but which is the essence of the teaching of all the great philosophers in Greece and in Germany: "We know that all things work together for good."[53] "The world-history is the purpose of God, which all in all is being fulfilled."[54]

I had also a kind of mystical belief that the great saints and prophets on the earth had understood this purposiveness of the world's history and been satisfied. I thought with Augustine of "that moment of Understanding which we longed for, which were the fulfilment of that promise, 'Enter thou into the joy of thy Lord.'" I had a curious experience about a year before meeting F.B. My friend M., mentioned above, tried to persuade me to come over with him one day to the theological college in the country where he intended to go on leaving Oxford. I said it would amuse me to see this new sort of Zoo, where all the prospective clerics were gathered together; I never missed a chance of jeering at M.'s future profession. The impression I got from my visit was not at all what I expected. I could not evade the feeling that these otherwise commonplace people had a secret resource somewhere, a certain

---

53 Romans 8:28 KJV "And we know that all things work together for good to them that love God, to them who are the called according to his purpose."
54 This seems to have come from Witness Lee (1905-1997), a Chinese preacher who followed Watchman Nee (1903-1972).

security about their life which it was a joy to feel.[55] I attributed the feeling rather unsuccessfully to the beauty of the place and the easy simplicity of their life; I knew that I had felt the breath of the Spirit of God. And I said, "How is it that the Christians have preserved something divine and living, in spite of their allegiance to a dead revelation and an obscurantist organisation—in spite of their immoral belief that a forgiveness of sins and benefits after death can be obtained through the recitation of some ill-understood formulae—in spite of their barbarous myth that God, to appease His own anger, demanded the sacrifice of an innocent person?" And I set to work furiously on comparative religion and mythology, on Frazer, and Reinach, and Rohde,[56] to prove to others and satisfy myself that all these Christian dogmas and rituals were old before Jesus appeared on the stage; that other religions had produced as high a morality and as high a culture; that the Christians could not claim a monopoly of the Divine Spirit, which had spoken from the poets and prophets and philosophers of every age.

One Saturday night I was writing an essay upon the idea of the soul, which I had been trying to trace through the early stages of European culture, when J. burst into my room, very excited. "Hello," he cried. "I've got a brand new phenomenon for you." He proceeded to tell me about F.B.

"But what does he do?" I asked.

"Oh, he just goes around waking up the individual."

"Well, I don't want to see him then; I don't want to be vaguely enthused; there's too much of that about the world already."

"But he's a regular prophet; he believes actively in the Spirit."

---

55 BB, pg. 15, "The joy of living we really have, even under pressure and difficulty." Cf. BB pg. 128, 132, 164.

56 J.G. Frazer (1845-1941) is a well known anthropologist and scholar of religion and myth. His *Golden Bough* traces the history of myths and legends. Salomon Reinach (1858-1932) was a Jewish Frenchman who studied archaeology, and religious history. Erwin Rohde (1845-1898) was a philologist and a close friend to Nietzche, who he corresponded with. His major works were on Greek religious beliefs on the soul. The common denominator here is that they all studied religion and myth very closely, and scrutinized Christianity as another myth among others.

"Well, I don't believe he is a Christian then," I said; "the Christians have long put the Spirit away on the shelf; they bring Him out once a year on Whit-Sunday, and then forget about Him again."

He looked at his watch. "Well, this is Whit-Sunday," he said.

Later in the day I made my first acquaintance with F.B. "A horrid, bumptious American," was my inward comment when he came into my room, with an introduction from J. I had severe toothache at the time, and was having a nerve slowly killed, and was feeling very disagreeable. I asked him about his travels. He told me some of his "yarns." The general theme was that "crows are black the whole world over."

"But I don't feel conscious of any particular sin," I said. "I have heard this stuff from my youth, and it all seems so irrelevant. I wish I were capable of committing some really great sin. It's just lack of opportunity, or, still more, lack of imagination. Your 'interesting sinners' had to be born interesting. I dream and criticise and never get anywhere definite. If only one knew what one had to do. . . ." And perhaps my attention turned upon my own inner soreness, and I forgot that two minutes ago I had been trying to decide how to get rid of the man. I forgot the unpleasantness of his voice; in fact, he hardly seemed to be there; he seemed to feel my dissatisfaction with things too well; he was no longer a second focus of consciousness, but was somehow sharing in mine.

"You are disorganised," he said, "without a centre—'without Christ.'"

Another man came in on a casual errand. It was like the switching on of the lights in a cinema. One's mind is not adapted for working on two levels at once. The silent figure in the corner had somehow set it going on the lowest level; the superficial didn't come easily. My visitor saw, I think, my embarrassment, and soon left.

F.B. began to ask me about my life. I felt somehow that I was on my trial, though not that this American was in any way concerned in it. I answered coolly and clearly.

45

"Well, I'm pleased to have met you, Mr.—," he said, getting up,
...

Something overwhelming came over me. It was an insult to play with this man. . . .

. . . "And I also lie" I continued in my narrative. "That is, usually. For instance, what I told you five minutes ago . . ."

I felt somewhat paralysed, as do probably all irresolute people after having let loose the irrevocable, but profoundly happy.

"God told me," he said.

He told me about his listening to God and of the Bible as the mouthpiece of the living Spirit; of the guidance of Jesus Christ here and now in the everyday decisions of life. A riot of new possibilities began to break into the dimness of my mental outlook. I prayed rather definitely.

I walked to the gate with him; I was feeling elated as never before. "I seem to have lost control of myself tonight," I said; "how absurd all this will seem to-morrow!"

"You've heard about the seven devils," he said. "Get going at once."

I walked by the river with another in the early morning, and it was as when the morning stars sang together, but after breakfast the whole events of the night before seemed hardly credible. "He is a psycho-analyst," I said, "although I didn't notice any of their tricks. We'll see if his stunt with the Bible works."

I hunted out a Bible and turned up by chance the story of the paralytic man. "What does all the business about the forgiveness of sins mean? Which is easier to say . . .? 'But that ye may know that the Son of Man hath power to forgive sins.' . . . What about my toothache last night!"

I have dwelt on this first meeting rather because of its immediate strangeness than because of its results. For the first time in my life I had deliberately and gladly made a fool of myself before a perfect stranger. I had told him things I had never breathed to another; I had told him of all my laughable vanities and dishonesties that make the stuff of a man's most intimate life.[57] I put it all down to some uncanny personal quality of the man, some quasi-hypnotic influence. (I believe now that religion has nothing to fear in psychological explanations of the working of God, though these do not carry one very far.) I can only say that I was fairly on my guard against such influences, after what I had heard from J.; and I must emphatically deny, in view of what is said in some quarters against F.B., that I was in any particular trouble at the time.

"Psychological or not, is this experience the voice of God?" That was for me the question. I answered, hesitantly but decidedly, "No!" Any half-savage thaumaturge playing skilfully on the chords of the mind could awaken such a momentary emotion. And my prejudice against Christianity in general, and against the religion of the Protestant sects in particular, rose up like a mist.

I saw F.B. no more, but had an invitation from him some days afterwards to attend his "house-party" at Cambridge on August 6th. I was pleased to have a really good excuse for not going— two successive invitations in the South of England which would make a return to Cambridge impossible. But about August 3rd I received three letters, two saying that owing to unexpected illness my invitations had fallen through, one from F.B. saying that he was expecting me at Cambridge. I was very annoyed with the presumption of the man; I wrote and told him so. But my curiosity was too strong; I went.

I will confine myself to the subjective impressions I received at that "house-party." First, one must take into account the natural attractiveness of even a Cambridge college in the summer. Second, I was surprised by the personnel. They were a very mixed lot, with perhaps a preponderance of the "Rugger Blue" type of undergraduate, but they were very natural, and seemed to have left the clique spirit behind. There were there three other Americans apart from F.B., and they mixed up with the rest very creditably. The soul of

---

57 BB, pg. 75, "We pocket our pride and go to it, illuminating every twist of character, every dark cranny of the past. Once we have taken this step, withholding nothing, we are delighted."

the party, F.B. himself, was very unobtrusive. He refused to preside at any of the meetings, but one knew without looking for him whether he was there or not. One admired his seeming carelessness about the success of his show. It was a bold idea bringing two distinguished speakers on the first night, but it broke down our first shyness. One felt already that the "walls were shaking."

Only all that that phrase implies was at that time new to me. There was hardly a trace of the hard religious dogmatism which I had gone there to find; but in so far as there was, I could not feel it. I was absorbed in a new experience. I felt as if I was living upon a mountaintop[58] right up against the sky, with the other peaks near and naked against the sun—peaks which it would take hours to reach along the devious, man-made tracks across the valley. And there was nothing left but the claims of God and of the other man standing there before God. And I saw that it was the sins of our choosing, the fear and shame, with which we tie ourselves about, which prevent us from living always thus simply and nobly. I saw also that it was all these things which debar us from a living faith in God; that one can only trust a person from whom one has nothing to conceal; that only this faith in the tireless working of God in our lives could let loose our buried energies, could bring us to take risks with our wealth and reputation. "Sin blinds, sin binds"; it could hardly be put better than in this catchword of F.B.'s—Christianity not as imprisonment, but as a Liberation of the soul![59]

This is all too vague and subjective, and yet I must emphasise one point. I do not remember the substance of F.B.'s speeches; it was not that which counted. I could and did in the group-discussion argue quite coldly against some of the points which he or his supporters seemed to overemphasise. It was a particular individual experience which I have had but few times in my life, and perhaps never with the same intensity—the experience I have described

---

58 BB, pg. 12, "It melted the icy intellectual mountain in whose shadow I had lived and shivered many years. I stood in the sunlight at last." And pg. 14, "I felt lifted up, as though the great clean wind of a mountain top blew through and through."

59 BB, pg. 55 "Yet we had been seeing another kind of flight, a spiritual liberation from this world, people who rose above their problems."

above as "standing before God." Whatever I may subsequently think of F.B. cannot alter my conviction on this subject.

I walked up and down the Quad much of one night, pleading against the hardness of the tasks that were set me to do. I had to tackle my parents; I had to tackle a man I had known and feared at school, the last person in the world I would have chosen to talk to upon this sort of subject; I had to put myself to shame before certain members of the party. I had, beside the practical questions, the whole theory of this new *Weltanschauung*[60] to tackle. And I said, "This time I am sure it is God's doing, and that He won't let me down."

It was nearly a year before I saw F.B. again, a year of hopes and disappointments. I had immediately to face my home and family; I had to face some earnest Cambridge undergraduates who were conducting a missionary campaign in my little town, and who nearly drove me into the wilds of revolt again. I have found it hard to believe that the denunciation of one's fellow-Christians is not of the essence of Christianity; so much energy and enthusiasm are spent upon it. It is hard for us human beings, to whom accidents of personality count so much, to remember that it is neither Paul nor Apollos that matters, "but God that giveth the increase."[61] I heard many months afterwards that even this personal clash brought its harvest. Perhaps it is only through such clashes that we learn slowly and painfully to separate the essence of the teaching of Christ from the purely individual elements in the personality of the teacher. Personality, the medium of all religion, is by no means an unequivocal conception. It is a recurrent charge against F.B. that "his disciples" are excessively dependent on him, take their experience from him at second hand. In most respects, however, we can only picture our relation to Christ through the personal relationships that we have experienced ourselves. Such experience

---

60 *Weltanschauung* i.e. 'world-view' the term goes back to at least Kant, was popularized by Hegel, and written on by Dilthey. A loaded term with a long philosophical history.
61 1 Corinthians 2:3-8 "I have planted, Apollos watered; but God gave the increase. So then neither is he that planteth any thing, neither he that watereth; but God that giveth the increase. Now he that planteth and he that watereth are one: and every man shall receive his own reward according to his own labour."

should warn us not to expect to go too fast. When anyone has lived many years in mutual distrust of his fellows it is the work of a few hours,—maybe a single act of faith, of willingness to humiliate himself—and the other comes out to meet him, comes further than he had dreamed; but it is the work of months, maybe of years, in spite of the best will in the world on both sides, to wipe away all the effects. There is much to unlearn.

Those of us who were at Cambridge, and had felt there something new come into our lives, formed a little circle at Oxford with the object of keeping that spirit alive by maintaining touch with each other. Perhaps we were all somewhat discouraged by the meagreness of immediate result. We had to contend with the damp warmth of the Oxford atmosphere, spiritual as well as physical, which is the enemy of heroic resolutions. I had to contend with the comparatively hard and monotonous work of the last year before "schools" (the final examination), and with the excuse it afforded for "minding one's own business" unduly. I had shrunk before the thought of this year before "schools," with all my friends "gone down"; it was better than I could have imagined. This faith which I had caught a glimpse of opened both my eyes and my mouth. I began to learn that I was not the only unfortunate in the world. I slowly began to think of doing something for the people with whom I was brought in contact, instead of thinking only of getting something out of them. By looking on them as opportunities, in this way I began gradually to lose my fear of strangers, a fear which I had come to regard as inevitable. But also I discovered things that had been happening around me for two years without my having any notion of their existence. I began to see a little of the picture that St. Paul describes as the "whole creation travailing in pain,"[62] and to feel my helplessness before this fundamental fact of the world. The many people whom I came across "by chance," by following the indications of God's guidance, which were sometimes unquestionable, people who were for one reason or another almost losing hope, to whom I had to try to impart something of the faith I had caught sight of—this was sometimes the only thing in the world that kept up my own faith. This

---

62 Romans 8:22 "For we know that the whole creation groaneth and travaileth in pain together until now."

may read like *Pragmatism*; it appeared to me rather as the continual confirmation of a belief which I would gladly have disbelieved. I felt myself again and again before the question, "Am I willing to make a fool of myself for the sake of another?" Or, rather, I felt it not as a question, but as an order, in circumstances where I could see no reason for it; on the occasions when I obeyed it, timidly and half-heartedly, I never found the command unnecessary.

Also during this time I began to beat out a working theory to fit my experience. This came about probably through an old acquaintance but new friend among the undergraduates of my college. I had long admired his knowledge, but looked down upon his rather naive enthusiasms. I had thought him rather "bourgeois"—a snobbish term for something that is peculiarly uncongenial to the bulk of those who have suffered from a public school education. I discovered gradually the goodness of his heart. I do not mean in this connection that I took over his theories. He belonged to the respectable High Church of the seventeenth century and the older Tractarians; but he believed sincerely and actively in his Church, and was at all times ready to defend it. He had an immense and varied acquaintance, who laughed at him and loved him. In the course of discussion with him my ideas began to shape themselves. He formed one of a small group who met to discuss the Philosophy of Religion. Its regular membership consisted of a Roman Catholic, a Jew, a young Modernist theologian, two mild Agnostics, a very naive American Atheist, and a pious, rather narrow Nonconformist. But the lines were already laid for me. On my return from Cambridge in the summer my father asked me to read and criticise one of the books of essays which are the product of the very remarkable group of liberal Christians in Oxford who are associated with the name of Canon Streeter.[63] I did find in the works of this group a theory of Christianity which was compatible with freedom and progress of thought, and with the demands of practical experience.

From the theoretical standpoint I had always had two fundamental convictions upon the nature of the world. I was on the one

---

63 B.H. Streeter (1874-1937) was the Provost of Queen's College at Oxford, and wrote many books on the New Testament and religion, and the harmony of religion with science. He died tragically in a plane crash in Switzerland.

hand attracted by the newer Evolutionism of Bergson[64] and his disciples. From this source, but perhaps more from my anthropological reading, I thought of the world as an endless flux, in which no beliefs, scientific, moral, or religious, could survive more than a few hundred years. Such a view has a special attraction for our generation, the generation which has grown up in the war period and seen "the old faiths ruin and rend."[65] Positivism has never had such a slump in the intellectual world as at the present time. At the same time I could not help believing that this development had a Meaning, a Value, which was somehow related to our values; I could not banish from my mind the great assertion of the Idealistic tradition that "all we have thought or hoped or dreamed of good shall exist . . . when eternity reaffirms the conception of an hour."[66] But how to imagine the conjuncture of these two postulates of experience, how to picture a world in which all our beliefs are transitory and in which we yet can know that all our beliefs are transitory!

The notion of a self-revealing God, a God who, out of blindly reacting animals, is creating Personal Souls in his own image; of this world of pleasure and sin as an Education, in the sense of Stevenson's prayer;[67] of the revelation of this "mystery" through the incarnation of Christ, the "Logos"—all this was new and wonderful to me, and supplied a theoretical want no less than a practical. My mind leaped back to the later Epistles of St. Paul, where he develops this idea of "God in Christ reconciling the world to Himself," of Christ as the head of a body of creatures grown conscious of their Creator. This again connected itself with a host of mystical speculations which are the common property of our age—an age awaking to the importance of the Unconscious and to the multiplicities of Personality. I have found them

---

64 Henri-Louis Bergson (1859-1941) was a French philosopher, and he seems to be referring to Bergon's book *Creative Evolution*, in which vitalistic spirit, man's creative impulse, evolves over time. Influential on Proust, William James, and others.
65 The earliest we could trace this quote back to was G.W. Foote's 1882 book *Arrows of Freethought*.
66 Another Robert Browning poem, this one entitled "Abt Vogler."
67 Robert Louis Stevenson (1850-1894), author of the *Dr. Jekyll and Mr. Hyde*, moved his family to Samoa and wrote a book of prayers.

recently set forth by a German novelist, Gustav Meyrink,[68] in his book *The White Dominican.* I only wish to emphasise the fact that from the orthodox Christian point of view my theory was at that time, to say the least of it, deficient. The view of the Atonement to an angry God through a vicarious sacrifice, the view that treats the words of Christ as a Law and God as a policeman, was abhorrent to me. I was also not prepared to admit that the sin of individuals could disorder the plan of the universe. I felt that this latter was in conflict with all the postulates of theoretical activity, just as the former doctrines struck at the root of all practical activity. In regard to the reality of sin, I would only go as far as Cleanthes'[69] prayer: "O God, let me follow out Thy will gladly; for if through evil desire I struggle against it to my own sorrow, yet must I follow it none the less." Sin harms the individual soul of the sinner; it cannot harm God, nor, if this seem paradox, can it harm other souls. Perhaps it was the inherited Calvinism of my fathers coming to the surface. Calvinism can be a very unattractive doctrine, but the notion of the overruling power of God to which it holds fast is of the essence of all religion whatever. It was the overwhelming belief in the power of God here and now[70] that inflamed the saints and prophets and heroes from the beginning of time. Was it possible to have a faith which could be progressive and liberal, and yet possess the power to move mountains? I believed then that it was. Perhaps the existence of such a prophet in a prominent position in Oxford was the only ground I had then

---

68 Gustav Meyrink (1868-1932) was an Austrian author who wrote many novels, one of which was entitled *The Golem*, and retold the Jewish legend of the same name. His son was paralyzed in a skiing accident, and committed suicide at 24. He died shortly thereafter. He opposed World War One, and was prohibited during the Nazi years.

69 Cleanthes (331 BC – 232 BC) was a philosopher and a boxer who studied under Zeno. His hymn to Zeus includes a phrase "we are thy offspring" that is referenced by St. Paul in Acts 17:28 "for in Him we live and move and have our being, as also some of your own poets have said, 'For we are also His offspring'." This was a favorite verse of St. Augustine. The Big Book says on pg. 62, "First of all, we had to quit playing God. It didn't work. Next, we decided that hereafter in this drama of life, God was going to be our Director. He is the Principal; we are His agents. He is the Father, and we are His children. Most good ideas are simple, and this concept was the keystone of the new and triumphant arch through which we passed to freedom."

70 BB, pg. 16, "We have it with us right here and now."

for such a belief. My greatest debt during this time is owed to Dr. Selbie,[71] although he was then unknown to me personally. His was the voice of one who, like Plato's philosopher-king, had climbed to the heights, without losing his bearings when he returned to the valleys. He was so unlike F.B. in every way, and like him in one respect—his religion was *alive*.

Thus, though not unconscious of my theoretical differences from F.B., it was this unmistakable living quality in his religion that made me await his return with eager expectation. Here was a man who could stir even Oxford. He did. How I am at a loss to explain. He sat for two weeks in a room in one of the colleges, and by the end of his stay the college was ranged sharply apart in two camps—the pro- and anti-F.B.'s. He addressed a meeting in the college soon after his arrival, at which an influential section of the undergraduates came with a concerted scheme to "rag" this impudent American. And somehow they felt their witticisms out of place, and the attack fell rather flat. Perhaps it was just the quiet confidence of the man that his enemies could not help feeling. Or one may repeat a second-hand story of how he led a petulant committee up to the top of Shotover Hill and harangued them upon their sins, with the effect that they one and all tried to re-sign. His whole stay in Oxford was an incredible *tour de force*. Was it more than that?

That, in the nature of the case, can never be answered by a human observer. I believe he brought help and "Good News" to many. I think I was somewhat disappointed with the immediate results in the "test-cases" I had mentally set him. You cannot write answers on a human personality as on a piece of foolscap. And I found it a little hard to answer the charge that much of his fol-lowing was obtained by the questionable method of making lurid confessions of sins in meetings. "Can this gospel be of God, if it be spread by playing upon the fears of the nervous and inexperi-enced?" This was the question that many people whom I respected put to me at that time. I had doubts like the rest, but I had op-portunities of knowing him more intimately than the rest. My

---

71 William Boothby Selbie (1862-1944) was Principal of Mansfield College, Oxford. He likewise wrote many books, on theology, the Bible, English sects, and several volumes of sermons and addresses.

mockery faded away into self-reproach at the first contact with his simple goodness. My natural embarrassment at being mixed up with this crank preacher at all was a spur to me to defend him more vigorously. I attributed all my doubts to the misrepresentations of his disciples.

His disciples? Perhaps therein lay the false conception that was the cause of my difficulties. It is easy to feel the emotion behind the great hymn of St. Francis, difficult to live it out in everyday life: "Let the Lord God be praised in all His creatures."

Is it possible in the last resort to distinguish Christianity from the opinions and prejudices of all other Christians whatever, without one's own belief becoming thereby thin and ineffective? My belief in Christ began to detach itself gradually from my belief in F.B. A few days' stay with my friend in his theological college mentioned above brought to my consciousness the fact that this Christianity had gnawed its way into my life. One morning in a wood on top of the Chilterns I felt irresistibly that Christ was calling me to some definite work. What it might be I had no idea. I was afraid before this "amaranthine weed."[72] Also I knew the vagueness and ineffectiveness of my temperament, to which F. B. was like a cold bath. With all this in mind, I accepted an offer of his to travel round Europe with him in the summer as tutor to a friend of his. I said I should go un-reservedly under his orders, under a vow of "holy obedience." It should be the discipline that was the essence of "Continuance."[73]

The second house-party was a foretaste of the continental pilgrimage; indeed, I met there most of the personnel of the "F.B. troupe"—as an observer once called it—for the first time. The atmosphere was not at all like that of the Cambridge party of the year before; the element of the professional Christian who has a pet doctrine to expound was much more in evidence. The first two days were peculiarly inharmonious; criticism was in the air. I found much that was uncongenial to me in the views and man-

72 From the 1890 poem "Hound of Heaven" by poet Francis Thompson.
73 The Oxford Group developed the "4 Absolutes," Absolute Honesty, Absolute Purity, Absolute Unselfishness, and Absolute Love; and the "5 C's,: Conviction, Confession, Contrition, Conversion and Continuance. Continuance can be seen as analogous to the 10th step of AA, taking inventory daily.

ners of the "disciples," but at the same time I discovered ever new qualities to admire in the "master." He had hardly spoken in the first two days, but he knew what we were saying, and was quite unperturbed by it. "*Wait*" I said to his detractors, "wait till he really takes things in hand."

The end of the house-party was the greatest personal triumph for F.B. that could have been imagined. The lion lay down with the lamb. It will have been adequately described elsewhere in this book. I went away, after lunching with a man I had once described as "the most unsympathetic I could imagine," with the voice that Peter heard sounding in my ears: "What God hath cleansed, that call not thou common."[74]

The "Continental tour," which gave me the most adequate insight into the personality and work of F. B., is difficult for me to describe in any detail, because it involved rather intimately the affairs of others, which I do not feel justified in bringing into print. It was a very severe lesson in practical internationalism. The "troupe" were all Americans[75]—which, however, should not be taken as a sufficient description of them. We had one other Englishman with us, a former acquaintance of mine, who joined the party as it was leaving England under somewhat peculiar circumstances. He was always there under protest, had considerable powers of observation, and used to turn the tap of his rather venomous humour continuously upon the Americans and their friends. I was always told off to look after him, and he was a great strain upon my loyalty to F.B. I was in a sense the cause of his joining the party. I had introduced him to F.B. because I believed he was in need of something that F. B. could give him. I cannot leave D. altogether out of the story, because he was in some sense one side of myself —the side that rebelled against the particular religious forms of the Americans. To explain what I mean I must introduce an idea which was very well expressed to me by a German friend: "You English," he said, "are always at the mercy of your 'Æsthetic Conscience.' You have an instinctive reaction against some forms

---

74 Acts 10:15 KJV "And the voice *spake* unto him again the second time, What God hath cleansed, *that* call not thou common."
75 (Original author's note) The host, I understand, was a very original and hearty Canadian, who not only paid the piper but set the tune. H. B.

of behaviour which seem out of place, vulgar, theatrical. This Æsthetic Conscience is right ninety-nine times out of a hundred; in the hundredth case it will prevent you from helping or appreciating a man whose constitution or education are radically different from your own." My Æsthetic Conscience had a hard time of it with the Americans. I was not accustomed to the ways of the sort of international hotels where Americans visiting Europe stay; to travelling round chateaux at the rate of half-a-dozen a day, counting them up as if they were scalps; to the habit of trying to buy any pretty thing that one caught sight of in a private house or garden. My tutorial work never materialised.[76]

If it had not been for D.—my departure would have left him in a peculiarly awkward position—I should have packed up and left the party. I felt myself in an alien culture, and it was quite clear that the other members of the party felt the same of me. I hardly saw F. B.; plans were made and changed over my head; I was physically tired with the perpetual travelling, and felt utterly in the dark. For the sake of D. I had to keep up my spirits and the honour of F. B. I spoke of the Diversity of Manners and the Identity of Principles. I was aware of the great complex of prejudices which I have called the "Æsthetic Conscience"—all too aware of it. I had lost confidence in my own values. I found myself in a state of utter bewilderment at the utter relativity of things. I said one day gravely enough to a German friend, who in a fit of absence of mind had poured sugar instead of salt on his egg: "I see it is the custom of your country to eat sugar with your eggs." That was what I felt like with the Americans. A severe disappointment over "schools" a couple of weeks before had completed my discouragement. I felt I *was* inefficient according to the American hustling standards, and the knowledge made me more inefficient than ever. F.B. never missed an opportunity of pointing out the fact to me. I told him once that living with him involved running one's head up against a stone wall whenever one tried to exercise any initiative of one's own; the only possible course was to follow orders passively. He used to lecture me with perfect justice on my "obtuseness"; he did really increase my powers of observation. He was too infallible; I wondered at the cleverness and the energy of

76 BB, pg. 84, "They will always materialize if we work for them."

the man; I began to feel more and more alienated from him.

And then a wonderful day came. We had just arrived in Brussels. The journeys always made me feel irritable. I had made up my mind to go at any price. Things were simplified for me. D. was so unusually rude to F.B. that it was decided that he would have to leave the party. I was "detailed" to take him on with me to my destination in Germany. I had a weary day trying to make plans for D. I came to see F.B. in the evening to make final arrangements. He was in bed. I thanked him formally for all he had done and told him what I meant to do.... And he looked at me very much moved, and said: "Clive, I have one thing to say to you before you go. I have got to ask your pardon. I've left you in the dark and in the cold. I'm sorry." ... I was overwhelmed; this from my superman? Anything but this. And he began to pour out all his hopes and anxieties, his plans and his disappointments. "No, no," I said, "you don't know, you don't know how I have suspected you and slandered you. ... If I had only known . . ." My stone wall had become suddenly human. *Become?* My mind went racing backwards over our travels, and I saw that there was no change in *him*, but an opening of my eyes to a side of him that had got lost in the press of an American holiday. We talked long and came to the roots of things. And I came to recognise for the first time the place of the human Jesus in the Christian world-order.

I saw F.B. later that night. It was about half-past twelve, and he looked very tired. He was going to talk with a man. I knew something about the business; it was a fight for an almost desperate soul. He told me something about it, and asked me to pray for him. I saw from his face what it meant to him. I think I understood for the first time something of what it meant to Jesus when the three disciples went to sleep in the garden. I prayed as never before to the Man of Sorrows, the Revelation of the loving pity of God.

I did not leave next day. We parted fittingly one sunny morning among the Bavarian hills, our hearts full of the splendour of the greatest drama in the world whose power glows from the faces of the peasant-players and draws spectators from every quarter of the world, without distinction of race or sect. One is a little conscious of the mechanical triumph of the stage Crucifixion, but in spite of it there is something there that awakes all the dramatic instincts in players and spectators, because it appeals to the most primitive and vital human emotions—the spectacle of a divine man taking leave of His friends and going consciously and in full faith to His death.

Since then I have had no occasion to change my mind on this fundamental point. I believe utterly in F.B.'s dictum, which indeed is not F.B.'s—"Look after the Practice and the Theory will look after itself";[77] "If any man do My Will, he shall know of the Doctrine."[78] But I do not believe that the two can be permanently kept in water-tight compartments. I have had some interesting experience since then which has increased my distrust of religious short cuts. I do *not* regard as short cuts the essentials of F.B.'s practice—the practice of scrupulous self-discipline as a means of keeping in touch with God and getting into touch with men; I regard them as necessary preliminaries for finding the way at all. But I believe fundamentally that the world is a process of being saved, of coming gradually through hard work to a knowledge of the Truth, the "Truth which shall make you free." I do not believe in the mechanical repetition of pious formulae about the Atonement or anything else. That belief may come. My future is uncertain enough. And I do not believe in any religion which shuts the doors of Development.

And F.B.? He is one of the greatest forces of good in the world at the present time. He is perhaps the most "real live" Christian that I have ever met. . . .

---

77 BB, pg. 86, "It works, if we have the proper attitude and work at it." Several AA cliches reinforce this point: "it works if you work it," "bring the body, and the mind will follow," "just do the footwork, and stay out of the results," "just do the next right thing," "keep your side of the street clean," "you can't think yourself into right action, you have to act yourself into right thinking," and etc. The basic point is on action, not theory.

78 John 7:17 KJV "If any man will do his will, he shall know of the doctrine, whether it be of God, or whether I speak of myself."

CHAPTER IV
A RUGGER BLUE

SHORT, thick-set, with a disproportionate breadth of shoulder, you would never think that this young Irishman had a turn of speed which made him famous at football. Nor on a first acquaintance would you be at all likely to think of him as one who took religion seriously.

A lively mouse-like brown eye lights up a broad good-natured face, while a smile as wide as lips can make it adds constantly a touch of whimsical mental quickness to the mere structural good-nature. He is one who loves lounging in a chair, who wears prodigious woollen waistcoats in winter, who gets his coat into rare disorder whenever he puts his hands in his trouser pockets, who listens lazily, who walks slowly, who speaks with an effort, but who laughs instantly, and with a lighting up of the whole face, at a good retort or a neat witticism, making you feel that he is always on the look-out, gratefully, for occasions of laughter.

I had met him before the house-party came together, and I saw him after the guests of that party had gone their several ways to nearly every quarter of the world. It was, therefore, quite easy for him to tell me his story and to answer my questions.

He said that his father, who is a fine, handsome Irishman, belongs to those who have a Church and State religion. It would be impossible for these people, he said, to imagine a Church without a State. Their religion is part of their politics, part of their class feelings. "My father," he related, "never spoke to me with the least intimacy about religion. His exhortations consisted of a friendly smack on the back, accompanied by the admonition, 'Keep straight, old man,' as if that could do any good to a fellow up against it. All the same, he was extremely kind, and a good sportsman. We liked him well enough."

His mother presents a more difficult problem for his autobiography. What can he say of her? To begin with, she was a wonderful, an altogether adorable person—loving beauty, loving fine poetry, devoted to animals and birds, making God perfectly real to her children, so that none ever doubted His existence for a moment; mystical, too, speaking to her children of "the Presence of Christ in the midst of the world," teaching them so convincingly about that exquisite moral life that they came to think of religion as "helping others"; yet, somehow or other, leaving this son, who adored her, who was devoted to her, very completely in the dark about vital matters, leaving him, as he says, to find out things for himself, and to suffer a good deal of avoidable pain in the process.

"When she spoke about the Presence of Christ," he told me, "I hadn't the ghost of an idea what she meant. I just felt it was something beautiful, like the sound of wonderful words in the poetry she read to me. She certainly did succeed in making the idea of God real to all of us. But it was the idea of a God rather a long way off, and rather overwhelmingly too almighty for our affection. I used to think of Him as One to whom I owed obedience, and who knew what I was doing, and who could be hurt or displeased when I wasn't doing my best. Still, it was a good, useful idea; and it was mixed up in some way with the beauty of the earth, which we all greatly appreciated, and the wonders of nature, which filled us with a good deal of curious admiration. In this way one had some sort of standard in one's mind, something at least to look up to."

When his moral struggles began, they found him wholly ignorant of their origin and significance. He was a little boy at school, pugilistic and keen on games, cheerful and larky, always ready for springing a joke. This strange black cloud slowly gathering over his mind, darkening the outer world, giving him a haunted feeling inside, troubling his brain and making his heart feel like a bruise—whence did it come, what was its meaning?

All he knew, by instinct—surely a strange instinct worth thinking about—was that this urge of his being in a particular direction had to be resisted. It was something against him. It was something of which the mere disposition made him ashamed. He felt as if he had been caught doing something underhand. "But the fight was the very devil, and at times I was more than disheartened—I was pretty sick of myself."

This struggle occurred at Rugby. It lessened as he moved up in the school. His last year was passed in a cleaner atmosphere. He never heard one whispered nastiness, never listened to tale or rhyme which could distress him. He was then nearly nineteen years of age, working hard for Cambridge. But the war, which was dragging on into its fourth year, did not come to an end, and away he went to be a soldier. His nineteenth birthday was spent in khaki.

He described this experience of the Army as "a pretty good shock." It taught him for the first time, he told me, "what the world was like." He added with a smile, "Nothing has ever surprised me since that time."

The horror was so great as to be grotesque—as to be comical, laughable. It was like seeing oneself for the first time in a distorting mirror. He cannot help smiling as he speaks of the upside-downness of that moral experience. He found himself among men who were frankly, freely, unfeignedly bad; who did beastly things with their whole will; who used the foulest language imaginable because they really relished words with that particular sound; who never tired of crude stories and dirty limericks; who were by nature, inclination, and election coarser and more filthy than any animal of the field; who were by nature, inclination, and election contemptuous of all refinement, all beauty, and all virtue—men whose idea of "a good time" was everything bad, men whose idea of "a bad time" was everything good.

To the Rugby schoolboy this atmosphere was sufficiently repulsive to save him from contamination; but his natural friendliness to all sorts and conditions of men, his disposition to take life as he finds it and never to set himself in any way above his fellows, might have had ill consequences for his moral peace had he not found in the Army two men as clean-minded and right-hearted as himself. "Religion saw me out," he said; "but, all the same, one couldn't go through that experience without a change. It made a difference to me."

Released from the Army, he went up to Cambridge. The atmosphere of the University at this time of stir and transition, he found, resembled that of the Army. Undergraduates were soldiers, not schoolboys. But there was a vital difference; men discussed other things besides vice. In his own set, he told me, "fellows were trying to find a way out." There were discussions on the subject. Some were for cold baths, others for physical exercises, and a few were advocates of developing will-power.

"So far as my own set was concerned," he related, "public opinion was healthy. Men who went up to town for adventures were regarded as contemptible. The long-haired, aesthetic type went in for vice, but the athletic type didn't. In the Army, vice of almost every kind was considered natural. At the Varsity there was a vicious type, and that sort of person was looked upon as a degenerate. The feeling among my set in Cambridge was something like this: We know this is wrong; how are we to get out of it? When we succumbed to temptation we were sick with ourselves. But we had sufficient courage to talk the thing over afterwards. We didn't bottle it up, and pretend we kept straight all the time. The thing was too unpleasant for that. We all wanted to be right, and therefore we sometimes discussed over our pipes how we were to dissipate the inclination which clamoured so terrifically for expression. It was with us rather like a discussion about getting fit for a race or a football match. We always looked at it from the point of view of physical fitness. Self-respect came into the matter, although we did not discuss that point of view; I suppose it was taken for granted; what came chiefly into the open of our talks was the confounded interruption which this thing introduced into our lives. It was a nuisance, like often catching cold, and a particularly beastly nuisance."

What strikes him in looking back to those days is the strange fact that there was no one to help them. Cambridge is full of churches and clergy, but no aid came from that quarter. The University shepherds altogether ignored this suffering of their flocks. No doctor ever lectured on the subject, no moralist offered a word of advice. The young men were left to fight the matter out among themselves, chiefly in secret.

He does not mean to suggest that particular notice should be paid to this driving temptation of youth; he is the last person in the world to desire a concentrated attention on such a matter, for that might easily become unhealthy. But he thinks the family doctor should provide the schoolboy with an explanation of this physical disturbance, warning him of the consequences of yielding to its urge and giving him a few notions about cleanliness, physical exercise, and sleep. In particular, he is now persuaded that if religion did its normal work, youth would have absolute power over all temptations that assaulted and hurt the soul, and this without any direct mention of sexual appetite.

While he was at the top of his form as a Rugby football player, as popular a man as ever played for his University, he was overtaken by a serious illness which brought him to death's door. It was impossible for him to face an English winter. He went first to the South of France and often into Italy, reading philosophy for his degree, and sadly lamenting his loss of the Rugger captaincy—a bereavement for which philosophy provided no consolation. In this period of lassitude, weakness, and disappointment, the old enemy awoke and tortured him worse than before.

He returned to Cambridge in order to take his degree, and, still fighting his moral battle, felt nevertheless that he was fighting a lost cause. The attacks were more frequent, the victories fewer. "I don't think," he says, "that I ever actually despaired; but I certainly had the distinct feeling that I was going downhill—morally, physically, everything. When a fellow gets to the point of feeling that it's not much good fighting he's in a pretty bad way. When he feels that he is going downhill, and that nothing can stop him, he's as good as done for. My state was something like that."[79]

One day, in this pitiful condition of mind, he went to call on a Rugger friend in another college, and there, for the first time in

---

79 BB, *Foreword to First Edition*, pg. xiii, "We, of Alcoholics Anonymous, are more than one hundred men and women who have recovered from a seemingly hopeless state of mind and body." And BB pg. 24, "At a certain point in the drinking of every alcoholic, he passes into a state where the most powerful desire to stop drinking is of absolutely no avail."

his life, came upon F.B., who made an immediate impression upon him—the impression of "a good fellow who knew how to put up a fight." They did not speak of religion or of ethics, but the conversation was of such a nature as made our young Irishman feel certain that F. B. could help him. When he got up to go he walked over to F.B.'s chair and said to him, "Look here, I'm going to look you up one day." "Do," said F.B., and they parted.

This is how the Rugger Blue tells the rest of the story. "F.B. never pursued me. But I couldn't shake the thought of him out of my mind. I got no line from him, never heard a word about him, never met him. Yet, from that moment of our first meeting, he was hardly ever out of my thoughts. I've talked to other fellows since about their first impressions of F.B., and I find that he took many of them as he took me. It was a strange strong feeling that he really knew about one, and could help one; that he had the right medicine, and could effect a real cure.

"At last, sure that this feeling was true, and absolutely wretched about myself, I got hold of F.B.'s address and went off to see him. He was out. I wanted to see him so badly that I sat down at the table in his room and began writing him a letter. All of a sudden he bounced into the room, breathlessly. 'I knew there was someone needing me,' he said. It turned out that he was on his way to see somebody else when he felt himself stopped dead in the street and *ordered* to go to his room. The other appointment was important, so he had run all the way back.

"I stayed ten minutes. We never got near what I wanted to say; there was a feeling of haste in that meeting; but I made it plain that I wanted to have a talk with him on a private matter, and he promised to come to my rooms in Trinity on the approaching Sunday evening.

"That evening was the turning-point[80] in my life. F.B. arrived between eight and nine. There was a most beautiful sunset;[81] the room was filled with its soft light. He sat with his back to the open window. I was facing him, looking over the dark outline of

---

80 BB, pg. 59, "Half measures availed us nothing. We stood at the turning point."
81 BB, pg. 54, "And then, with a better motive, had we not worshipfully beheld the sunset, the sea, or a flower?"

his head to John's Church, with its cross shining against the glow of the setting sun. It was an extraordinarily still evening. F.B. seemed to me a part of its stillness. He wasn't in one of his cheerful moods. He hardly said a word, and what he did say was said in a very subdued tone of voice. I sat looking at the cross against the sky, wondering how the devil I was to tell this man, whom I scarcely knew, things about myself which sickened me, disgraced me in my own eyes. Somehow or another, I can't tell how it was, the sight of the cross in the sunset, so high up in that wonderful air and yet not in the least distant from my own darkness, gave me a kind of headlong courage. Before I quite knew what I was doing I said to him, 'Well, I may as well tell you all about it.' He said, 'Go on,' and waited for me to continue. I knew then, absolutely, and with a regular blaze of certainty, that he could clean me out. I told him the whole trouble, everything.

"I had discussed this thing often enough, but I had never before confessed it. With other fellows I had spoken of myself as a physical problem, going over symptoms, leaving them to infer the actual tumbles; but here, for the first time in my life, I had torn up my moral life by the roots and held it out to another man. The feeling of this was not, as I should have thought, one of shame and disgrace, the bitterest humiliation a decent fellow can experience; on the contrary, it was one of tremendous relief. That in itself surprised me. I had the distinct sensation that one gets in dropping a heavy load from the shoulders—a feeling of expansion and lightness. I remember, too, that I felt as if something which I had kept bottled up inside me ever since I could remember anything was gone, clean gone. You see, I had been feeling fairly desperate, and that made me, once I got started, careless of what I said; I didn't mind what I told him; everything came out, everything I loathed and hated in myself, and in coming out it seemed to stay out.

"F.B. never spoke a word. I couldn't see his face against the light, and I couldn't tell how he was taking it, and I don't think I very much cared. I wound up in a natural way by telling him that I'd tried athletics, that I'd gone in for all sorts of exercises, cold baths, and tricks for strengthening the will, but in vain. I was going downhill in my thought life; what was I to do? Did he know a cure? Would he advise me?

"Then F.B. told me everything."

Three particulars in that "everything" seemed to have brought instant illumination to the mind of this undergraduate. First, that moral chaos is inevitable when there is no singleness of mind; second, that the power which purifies, strengthens, and upholds can only become real to those who long for it, and open the doors of their cleansed hearts to receive it in silence; and third, that no soul, truly conscious of that power, can be satisfied with its own salvation. "If you sit still," he said, "it's hopeless; help other men."[82]

That was the supreme test. A man could easily prove for himself whether he had genuine singleness of mind, genuine contact with the divine power. All he had to do was to consider his attitude towards other men. Did he want to help others? Had he something in himself which could help them? It was no use pretending in this matter. No help could come to a soul that didn't really want it. No purity could come to a heart that prayed for it, "but not yet." No power could come into a life that was selfish.

"*Sin blinds, and sin binds.*" Be careful. Think those two words over—*blinds and binds*. Don't be quite sure that what you think you see is the truth. Don't be quite sure that you can really do what you like. Cross-examine yourself.[83] You may be blind. You may be a slave. While sin is in your mind you are not a free creature, you are not a seeing creature. Sin is self; while it is there in the mind, whatever form it takes, a man may deceive himself to his life's end, may even go so far as to believe that he is good, that he is serving

God, that he is helping other men. But he isn't. Sin walls God out. "Then will I profess unto them, I never knew you."[84] An awful sincerity, a sincerity that searches every crack and corner of the

---

82 BB, pg. xxxi, "The patient had made his own diagnosis, and deciding his situation hopeless, had hidden in a deserted barn determined to die." Cf. pg. 20, 42, 44, 92, 94.

83 12&12, pg. 51-52, "But all alcoholics who have drunk themselves out of jobs, family, and friends will need to cross-examine themselves ruthlessly to determine how their own personality defects have thus demolished their security."

84 Matthew 7:23 KJV. "And then will I profess unto them, I never knew you: depart from me, ye that work iniquity."

human heart, is necessary if God is to enter—the living and the Eternal Righteousness.

Many believe that when they pray for purity they really and truly want to be pure. They deceive themselves. It is a mere passing emotion. The root of the sin is still in their hearts. Two things must go together—a deep and passionate hatred of sin, a deep and passionate craving for God.

Ask—with singleness of mind—and it shall be given you; seek—with singleness of desire—and ye shall find; knock—with singleness of purpose[85]—and it shall be opened unto you. A good tree cannot bring forth evil fruit, neither can a corrupt tree bring forth good fruit.

The reasonableness, the inexorable justice of this teaching, brought instant illumination to the soul of the young Irishman, and he took that plunge away from self which baptises the spirit of a man in the living waters of eternal life. He really wanted the touch that makes personality a whole.

He said to me that so wonderful was his belief that he set about "tackling other men" almost at once. He told those men what F.B. had told him, and recommended them to try what he himself was trying, F.B.'s method of rising early in the morning to be alone and silent with the thought of God in the soul. He told them that in these times of silence he had learned to relax his whole body, and that with so simple an invitation as, "God, come into my soul, and help me," evil thoughts drained clean out of him, and he really did become vitally conscious of invisible power.[86]

All this he did in so masculine and sincere a fashion that a group soon formed in his room of men who really longed for spiritual life—a life which they could not find in the formal ritual, however beautiful, of churches and chapels. F. B., who realised the

---

85 'Singleness of Purpose' was a phrase used by Bill Wilson in a 1957 talk, and has since become a common phrase within AA. It is synonymous with the "primary purpose" of the 5th Tradition. The 12th step suggests a single purpose for those who have recovered—to carry the message and help others.
86 BB, pg. 85, "We have begun to develop this vital sixth sense."

remarkable power of this man to influence others, soon afterwards sent him over to Oxford, where his twin brother was at Balliol, in order to begin there a similar work of personal religion.

The Balliol brother invited a few men to his room and the Cambridge brother talked to them. One of these men came from Christ Church; he was impressed, and suggested a somewhat bigger gathering at the House.

"It was there," says the Rugger Blue, smiling, "that I made my first speech. It was pretty rotten. The room was full of scholars, and I felt as nervous as a cat. But after I had got through they took the matter up in discussion, and we debated it from pretty nearly every angle till the small hours. What struck them most, I think, was the reasonableness of F. B.'s idea that the measure of help is the measure of desire. They never flinched or jibbed at this idea because it is just. Theological difficulties were hardly mentioned; the centre of discussion was how to get the heart honest in its desire for the right thing.[87] We talked and talked till the moon was high in the sky. Then we went out into the Quad, and walked round and round the fountain, still talking. I had a fellow on each arm. Sharing a trouble makes friends. The feeling that you can help another fellow is one of the best in the world. We were tremendously happy. They came to see me in my rooms. We made a compact which still holds good. Wonderful things have come of that visit."

Later on, during the Long Vacation, the Rugger Blue arranged a house-party in Cambridge, so that a number of men should meet F. B. and discuss the whole question of personal religion.

He gave me a characteristic account of that gathering. "I don't suppose I've got much of a reputation for tact," he said, smiling broadly; "in any case, I never stopped to think how the people I asked would mix.[88] The thing was to get a lot of interesting fellows together, and leave F. B. to do the rest. The consequence was we had a party of thirty men—Indians, Yanks, Japanese, Chinese,

---

87 The 3rd Tradition of AA is "The only requirement for A.A. membership is a desire to stop drinking." Cf. also pg. 95, "If he is to find God, the desire must come from within."

88 BB, pg. 17, "We are people who normally would not mix."

Oxford, Cambridge, business men, Members of Parliament, and one or two howling swells from the War Office. It was most amusing. You saw Etonians in white spats talking to prospective socialistic curates! And there was extraordinary cordiality. Everyone was interested. It seemed as if they had all been life-friends. I never knew such a lack of strain in any gathering of men. We kept it up for several days. We got right down to bedrock—the need for absolute uncompromising, all-out sincerity. And I'm perfectly certain of this, that every man there was helped. Out of that party grew the party you came to; and we've got another coming on in a month's time at Cambridge; and after that some of us are going to Universities in Germany, and some to Universities in the United States."

The last time I saw him was at Talbot House, in York Road, Lambeth, happy in the midst of very lively youth. He has decided to be a doctor, and when he has taken his medical degree he is going to attach himself to the Talbot House Movement, placing himself and his services entirely at the disposal of that very noble fellow, P. B. Clayton, M.C., the adored chaplain of Poperinghe, to do what he can to help young men through every illness of soul and body.

CHAPTER V
PERSONA GRATA

WHEN the house-party gathered together he was crossing the Atlantic, but long before he arrived the English garden in which we walked and debated grew well used to the sound of his name. I was assured that he was "an absolute topper." I was told that everybody loved him. Again and again he figured as the hero of a tale or the author of a good saying. The mention of his name always brought affectionate smiles to the faces of those who knew him.

Thus dangerously heralded, P.G.,[89] as I shall call him for brevity's sake and anonymity's sake, joined our party on the day before it broke up. I had the pleasure of hearing him make one very simple and modest speech, and the greater pleasure of taking a moonlight walk with him under the tall trees of that beautiful garden. We agreed together that he should pay me a visit in Dorsetshire before he returned to America. He kept that promise, taking my family by storm, and leaving behind him an impression which is still as gracious and fresh as the hour which brought him into our circle.

His gift of charm, I think, lies in a wholly unconscious retention of the graces of boyhood. There is no hardness in his character, no sense of firmness in his disposition, no hint of decisive energy in his mind. If he were a writing-man, Macaulay would frighten him and Lamb would be very dear to him.[90] Among the dogmatists he would be all at sea; among the men of "push and go" he would be trodden underfoot. He suggests to you that his mind is still full of wonder, like the mind of a child.

---

89 Despite some research, we could find no likely suspect for these initials. As such he remains anonymous.
90 Thomas Macaulay (1800-1859) was a poet and historian, as was Charles Lamb (1775-1834).

The memories of his defeats have left no bitterness; the remembrance of his victories has brought no sense of triumph. His pilgrim's progress, I think, has something of the radiance and innocence that we find in Bunyan's page.[91] Everything in his nature is modest, gentle, and sincere. He is in this world as a shy boy must be accounted one of the guests at a roystering party. You feel that he will never quite settle down, never come to feel that all this bustle and stir are in the true nature of reality. He sees something that the rest of us do not see, but is afraid to talk about it, lest he draw attention to himself. He makes you think of Mr. Dick without his delusion, or of William Blake[92] without his insanity. Every motion of his spirit is the expression of a profound and incorruptible simplicity—a simplicity so wholly unconscious that it makes everybody love him. Nothing in the least theatrical has ever brushed even the outskirts of his mind.

He spent his boyhood in a small American country town, characterised by all the respectabilities and pruderies of a thoroughly compromising civilisation, entirely without the inspiration of the great realities.

He was one of three children, and the only son. Between father and son, so far as religion was concerned, there was a wall, but between son and mother no obstacle of any kind. He believed everything she told him, and saw nothing in her life to criticise or to disturb his worship. She was orthodox, but not narrow-minded; he loved her completely.

The first incident in his spiritual life occurred when his elder sister, seven years older than himself, returned from college with a definite religious experience. This change in his sister enabled him to comprehend the difference between "first-hand and second-hand religion." He describes the change in his sister as the change from sleep to waking. Something of the same nature occurred in himself; he was no longer asleep, but could not feel himself properly awake.

91 John Bunyan (1628-1688) he served in the English Civil War on the side of Parliament, was imprisoned afterwards for 12 years for his preaching. He wrote *Pilgrim's Progress* in 1678, and it was one of the most popular books of its time. It was an allegory about spiritual development.
92 William Blake (1757-1827) was a poet, painter, and printmaker.

One thing greatly struck him in this transitional condition of mind—the visible fact that his sister's life was now "propagating in the lives of other people." This seemed to him a very wonderful thing, and the thought that it was possible for one person to make another person happy, to make an indifferent person active, and a bad person good, stuck in his mind.

But, though he took part in the religious activities of his school, he found that he didn't fit, that he wasn't in the least like his sister, and therefore he came to the conclusion that he was not yet properly awake. This idea of sleep and waking came to him with the simple naturalness characteristic of all his thinking. It was not an idea put into his mind by somebody else. He came of himself to think of people as asleep, half-asleep, half-awake, awake, broad-awake.

He seems to have passed through boyhood without moral disturbance of any kind. His one distress was the haunting thought that he could not establish a more real relation with the God of orthodox religion. But this thought was without distress. It rose into consciousness between periods of singular happiness, for he was a boy made for the delights of schooldays.

His battle began in his first term at college. He went to Yale, which is in New Haven, and for the first time in his life breathed the atmosphere of a town which had the flavour of a great city. All the placid provincialism of the little country town in which he had dreamed and mused away the years of boyhood was consumed in the rakish gaiety of this University town. A walk down Chapel Street was enough to set his head spinning. This street, with its fashionable shops, its numerous theatres, and its cosmopolitan restaurants, is a favourite parade for harlots and "adventure girls"—pretty girls from the chorus of comic operas, and girls of the town whose moral standards are on the same level as their standards in manners, literature, and art. The effect it makes on a provincial is one of rebuke; he is persuaded to feel that he is narrow, dull, wanting in spirit, a prisoner to fear, a captive of stupidity. The bright people smiling and laughing in the sunshine of that cheerful thoroughfare seem to flaunt a superior liberty and a higher courage in the dazed eyes of the youthful provincial.

They are not the victims of illusion; it is he, gaping at them, who is deceived. They are not going down to perdition; but he wanting to join, and yet afraid, is on the road to mediocrity.

Nothing in the religion of this boy was proof against the temptations of Chapel Street. For the first time in his life he experienced an uprush of those feelings which are so powerful to create the highest happiness of the human soul, so powerful to destroy the last rags of its liberty and self-respect. He was tempted, and the temptation seemed to foul his spirit. He could not withstand the call of apparent beauty and apparent gladness.

This tremendous pressure on his purity drove him to religion as a refuge. He describes it as a home to fly to while he was at college; a narcotic which brought relief; an argument, a persuasion, but not light.

On his way home at the end of his first term he passed through New York. There was a great storm crashing over the city, and he watched it with his thoughts set on his own burden. That burden, he says, was awful. He asked himself, Why isn't Christ personal to me? and in asking that question a sigh broke from his lips, and with the escape of that sigh something of his burden seemed to go. He felt that he had begun to get an answer.

When he returned to Yale it was with the decision to follow his sister's example, and "to propagate in other lives." The experience was disheartening. One of the students was very ill, perhaps dying, and P.G. went to see him. They talked together, but "I couldn't get through to him," he says; "there were barriers between us as big as mountains."

He spoke of another man he tried to influence. "This man," he said, "belonged to the type of attractive sinner—a delightful person, a man with personality; charming, with magic about him, lovable. He was intellectual, and could floor my persuasions with arguments gathered from history and human experience and science. He was quite friendly; he knew I cared for him; I think he liked me; and he was the kind of man who appreciated sympathy; but nothing I could say made the smallest difference to him. You see, what I was doing was to try to superimpose myself on other people; I was trying to do them good from a height on which I wasn't really standing.[93] That is fatal."

Intellectual difficulties presented themselves. Orthodox religion was exposed to the attacks of clever young men who knew more science than theology. There were, indeed, intellectual courses at the college which seemed to him directed against religion. He was shaken, but he suffered no mental anguish. Involved in theological disputes, he had nothing to say. He retired from them to read his Bible more industriously and to pray more earnestly for light.

His sympathy with men took him into all quarters. One night he found himself in a room full of rackety students, who presently began to tell coarse stories. P.G. rebuked them, opposed himself single-handed to the whole group. "I was dealing with symptoms, not causes,"[94] he relates, with a smile; "instead of opposing myself to the group, I ought to have waited and reasoned with individuals."

He had now made up his mind to attach himself to the Christian Student Movement in India. Temptation had eased. Prayer meant much more to him than it had ever meant in the past. Religion had at last become apparently real. Yet a trouble remained which preyed upon his peace of mind. "Religion was real to me," he says, "but I could not give it away."

He left the University and went out to India. For three years, loving his work, he remained in that country, forming, as he says, superficial friendships, but doing nothing really effective to stop the appalling vice which existed among young Indians.

He returned to America, and joined the famous seminary at Hartford, Connecticut. For a year he was profoundly happy. He loved his freedom, the peace of the seminary, and the long, unbroken hours of study. He thought he was fitting himself to be a teacher of the Christian religion.

---

93 BB, pg. 95, "Never talk down to an alcoholic from any moral or spiritual hilltop; simply lay out the kit of spiritual tools for his inspection."
94 BB, pg. 64," Our liquor was but a symptom. So we had to get down to causes and conditions."

The second year brought disillusion, and something akin to terror. Temptations assaulted him with a quite incredible force, a quite sickening persistency. Doubt, too, was for ever whispering to his conscience. He found that his heart was full of impurity, his mind as full of intellectual dishonesty. He was hedging, compromising, pretending. Rather than cause pain to others he felt that he must go on with the religious life; but it began to be to him a shadow, a phantasm, something out of a forgotten past that had no meaning for a present terribly and overwhelmingly insistent.

He said to me, "I really do not know any form of mental misery so tragic as the misery of the theological student—the afflicted disciple. The men in these colleges and seminaries are the hungriest groups in the world. They have good motives, but no direction. They are assailed by temptations which make them ashamed. They do things which choke them with a sense of self-contempt, a sense of hypocrisy. The atmosphere is more corrupting and damning than the atmosphere of Universities. One feels that these places are full of repression, full of unuttered sin. There's something furtive about them. You don't get public drunkenness, public gambling, public immorality. There's no visible and healthy clash of good and evil. Good is taken for granted, and absence of evil is also taken for granted. But the evil is there; and the good—well, it is not easy to feel its influence. As for the professors, their only experience of religion is a memory.

They tell the students what happened years ago, not what happened coming down in the tram, or in the home last night. They have no reality for these desperate students, who spend half their time studying the soulkilling controversies of long-ago theologies, and the other half in fighting temptations sharp as steel. People wonder at drunkenness and 'rags' among Varsity men; I think I know how those things come about. They are attempts to break away from repression, to escape from a maddening sense of conflicting duality."

One of the students at Hartford had been a miner and a sailor; he had made a fortune and spent it. He was about thirty-five years of age, and used to write sermons for the other students. He had a gift for preaching which created admiration among the younger men. P.G. liked this strange man and talked to him, tried to "get below the surface to the place where he lived." One day the ex-miner said to him, "Shall I tell you what I am? I'm a damned hypocrite. I've been twice with women quite lately."

P.G. had the terror always before his eyes that he too might fall. One night in New York he had to rush into the streets and walk as hard as he could go for miles, fearing that the temptation would beat him. He says, "I was a divided personality.[95] There were two of me; no unity. I felt that I might fall; yet I felt that nothing on earth should make me."

He was in this state of mind, seeing little hope before him of avoiding hypocrisy, when F. B. came to Hartford as an Extension Lecturer. His subject was, "How to deal with Other Men; how to get into their Lives." One day P.G. was walking in the grounds of the college when someone, coming up from behind, took his arm, and said, "This is P.G., isn't it?" P.G. turned to find F.B. at his side, smiling in the far-away manner which sometimes takes the place of his usual alertness. He began to speak of someone in India who had met P. G.

The immediate feeling of P.G. was one of conviction that he could speak with complete frankness and confidence to this stranger—stranger no longer, for the touch of his hand had conveyed an instant feeling of friendliness.

"I knew," he told me, "that here was a man of understanding sympathy, one who wouldn't be shocked, one who could help. Another thing I knew—that there was no professionalism about him, that he wouldn't think of me as 'a case,' that he was a genuine man genuinely interested in another man.[96] I remember, too, I had the feeling that in this man there was plenty of time. Nothing suggested commercial bustle. He seemed to me to be living in a

---

95 BB, pg. 21, "He is a real Dr. Jekyll and Mr. Hyde."
96 BB, p. 18, "That the man who is making the approach has had the same difficulty, that he obviously knows what he is talking about, that his whole deportment shouts at the new prospect that he is a man with a real answer, that he has no attitude of Holier Than Thou, nothing whatever except the sincere desire to be helpful; that there are no fees to pay, no axes to grind, no people to please, no lectures to be endured—these are the conditions we have found most effective."

wonderful spiritual leisure. We parted with nothing much said between us, but on the following day, after breakfast, he came and sat with me on the garden steps in the morning sun. For the first time in my life I told another man exactly how I stood, and something of what I had suffered. I turned to him and said, 'My mind is filled with a cloud of evil thoughts; why do I have these evil thoughts?' To my astonishment he said at once, 'Why, P.G., I have those evil thoughts,' as if he were surprised that they should worry me. Directly he said that I had the feeling he knew what to do with them. There was a deep sense of relief in my mind. He said nothing more to help me. All he added was that I must come to see him later in the day.

But I felt extraordinarily happy, just as if the fight was over.

"When we came to have our talk he told me that the reason I was tortured was simply because I was fighting temptation direct. The attempt at repression was the cause of my suffering. It was necessary for me to leave all such fatal egoism and to get out into the lives of other men—altruism, Christianity. He spoke quietly and convincingly. But I wanted it my own way, and comfortable; I didn't want to pay the price;[97] so I challenged him to tell me why I could not get relief in the old way, by prayer and reading the Bible. He told me that I had to get into the lives of other men, and that was all there was to it. Selfishness was my sin. I wasn't thinking of others.

"One day, shortly after this, I was walking in town with him when we came across two drunken men. He told me to take one while he took the other. I was paralysed by fear. I hid behind a telegraph-post. But F.B. collared his man and saw him home. Next day, in the midst of a meeting, F.B. had an irresistible impulse to go out into the street; someone there wanted him. He left the meeting, went out into the street, and there was the drunken man of last night. F.B. put that man on the right road.

"When he told me this I felt poverty-stricken. Religion began to seem to me something that was not natural. I should never be able to handle other men as F. B. handled them. I was like a young

97 BB, pg. 14, "Simple, but not easy; a price had to be paid. It meant destruction of self-centeredness." Cf. pg. 155.

surgeon with trembling knife confronting a new operation.

"I confessed this feeling to F.B., and he took me a step further; he taught me the principles of religion. He explained that I felt helpless because my religion was not in action. This meant that I had never experienced 'the expulsive power of a new affection.' If I had real love for men I should be willing to share my temptations with them, to confess to them my secret thoughts, to get alongside of their souls, to work with them and for them to the end of re- demption. Every man, he said, could test the reality of his religion by finding out whether he would make sacrifices to help others.

"I saw what he meant intellectually, but I didn't want to come to it. I told myself that there was something immodest in his suggestion, that my spiritual life was too sacred to talk about—as if anything is too sacred that helps other men! So I withstood him.

"One day he surprised me very much by saying that he was going back to China for six months and wanted me to go with him. I had another year to run at Hartford. China did not attract me. I'm not sure that F.B. attracted me. I rather shrank from his too personal methods. But he persuaded me, and those six months stretched into two years, and those two years are the happiest memories in my life.

"Before I left Hartford I decided to try F.B.'s method. I went to a theological student who seemed to me to be troubled, to be suffering, and confessed to him my own secret sin—impurity. The feeling of relief was extraordinary. The student came to life, con- fessed his secret sin to me, and ended our talk by saying, 'Prayer is going to mean something now; the Bible is going to mean some- thing now.' To both of us it seemed that religion had never been real to us before, never been alive, and that now it was the very biggest thing alive.

"The revelation came to me in this conviction: *God floods in when a man is honest.*[98] I had been looking at religion from the

---

98 BB, pg. 56, "In a few seconds he was overwhelmed by a conviction of the Presence of God. It poured over and through him with the certainty and majesty of a great tide at flood. The barriers he had built through the years were swept away. He stood in the Presence of Infinite Power and Love. He had stepped from bridge

intellectual point of view. I had never really seen it as the supreme power of morality. I had never really apprehended that religion redeems and dominates the sinful heart of man—not merely the sin of impurity, but the entire moral life—selfishness and all our moral hesitancies.

"I came to myself in confessing to another man, that is to say, in being perfectly honest. For the first time in my life I felt that there was no pretence in my soul, that another man whom I wanted to help knew me as I knew myself, and that I really and truly did want to help him—that I had torn away all pretensions in order that I might be able to help him.

"I am convinced that confession plays a tremendous part in religious life. I don't think it is too much to say that until a man confesses his sin to another man he can never really be spiritually vital.[99] One knows scores of men who carry guilty consciences, and who think they square accounts by confessing their sins in secret to God, and genuinely trying not to commit those sins again. Such men can never help another; such men haven't the ghost of an idea what redemption means. They pretend. Their religion is a form. Their life is a dead letter.

"An interesting story occurs to me. A friend of mine wanted very much to help a particular friend of his who was involved in some trouble with a girl. He tried and tried, in vain. He asked me why he couldn't do this thing. He wasn't lacking in sympathy; he wanted to help his friend; why couldn't he? I got him to go over his past life. He found that there was an un-confessed sin on his conscience. As a schoolboy he had stolen money from his father. It was a hard task, but he went to his father and confessed his sin. The result was not only ability to help his friend, but a real pentecostal joy in his own heart. He said to me, 'Now I'm ready to go all the way in this thing.' How simply a man can be born again! One act of honesty. Reality!"

Let me interrupt the narrative for a moment to remind the

---

to shore."
99 BB, pg. 73, "We think the reason is that they never completed their house-cleaning. They took inventory all right, but hung on to some of the worst items in stock."

reader that in Morton Prince's *The Unconscious*[100] many stories showing that some forgotten incident in the past, but not forgotten by the unconscious mind, may prey upon physical health and even be the cause of serious physical ills.

I remember one case in particular. A woman subject to epileptic fits was hypnotised by Dr. Prince, and taken back by him through all the days of her life in search for the shock which had deranged her mental processes. He discovered from her unconscious mind that once, as a little girl, she had been sitting alone in her nursery with a kitten in her lap, that this kitten had suddenly had a fit, that she had screamed for her nurse, terrified by the kitten, and that the nurse did not come for a very long time. The doctor awakened her from hypnosis, told her of this incident, of which she had no memory, and so disposed of the cause of her trouble. From this case it will be seen that even things which the conscious mind has forgotten may remain in the folds of being, festering the entire life.

Religion, one may observe, seems to have known by instinct what painful science is only now beginning to suspect. Always it has taught the need of confession, restitution, and a cleansed heart.

P.G., at any rate, is insistent on the power of confession to fill the spirit with an entirely new sense of life. He lays all his emphasis there. To him the matter is not in the least mysterious. Confession is merely a sign of an absolute honesty within, a sign that the long attempt to compromise and equivocate is over, a sign that the personality is at last unified, not divided, a sign that the soul really means what it says, and truly believes what it has hitherto only professed or tried to believe.

By confession he means no formal act of clericalism, performed to square accounts with the Deity,[101] but a most personal

---

100 Morton Prince (1854-1929) was a physician who specialized in neurology and helped establish psychology in America. He worked alongside William James and others, and helped characterize dissociative disorders. The book mentioned was one of many he wrote on the unconscious, dissociation, and personality.
101 BB, pg. 74, "Though we have no religious connection, we may still do well to talk with someone ordained by an established religion. We often find such a person

act on the part of one man to another—particularly to the man one is trying to help—an act that attests honesty and brings one man close to another, in sympathy and reality.

He is the more certain of the power of confession from his experience in the East. He told me that he found he could do nothing with men in China, Japan, and Korea until he persuaded them to confess their secret sins, but that directly this confession was made they experienced precisely the same joyous relief which he had experienced. The confessions of young men in China, Japan, and Korea, he says, fit perfectly in with the confessions of young men in England and America. He agrees with F.B., "Crows are black the whole world over."

"I saw many miracles in the East," he said to me, "and I am now seeing like miracles in America and in England. All the world over sin is darkening men's lives, and hypocrisy is paralysing the power of religion to save them. Religion is a universal force. It does not much matter, I think, what theological language is used to express the immense miracle of redemption. What matters is making it real to suffering men that directly they are absolutely honest in desiring release from the slavery of sin, God will flood into their hearts, and they really will be born again. Redemption *cannot* come, I'm perfectly certain of this, until the heart is so hungry for it that it will confess everything to another. One has to be awfully real oneself to experience reality.

"I remember a strange incident in China. I came across, in one of the mission colleges, a Chinese teacher who was a complete hypocrite. He drank, he gambled, and he had relations with married women. He was a man of some intellect and no little power. One night, sitting over the fire, he said to me, 'All this Christianity is a legend. Jesus, you know, is not an historical figure. I never say my prayers. I teach, because I can teach. But,' with a shrug of his shoulders, 'I do not believe what I teach.' I took no notice of his effort to get me into a theological argument. I spoke of the Christ of universal human experience, the Christ who saves, the Christ who redeems, the Christ who had made all the difference to me.

---

quick to see and understand our problem. … If we cannot or would rather not do this, we search our acquaintance for a close-mouthed, understanding friend."

He turned, with a strange light in his eyes, looking at me over his shoulder, his hands still extended to the fire, and 'How would I take that medicine?' he asked. I said to him, 'Will you pray from your heart, "Jesus, if there be a Jesus, I want you to clean me up"?' To my surprise, then and there, looking into the fire, he prayed that prayer. Then he got up and left me. The next day he came to me and said, 'You know, this thing works marvellously.' It was his first experience of personal religion. He had never before seen redemption as the central fact of Christianity. He said to me, 'Now I feel on top.' He had never before looked at religion as a real power that enters the heart, changes the life, and gives a new birth to the soul. I am quite sure he had never wanted to be cleaned up.

"What strikes me most in all these wonderful experiences—for it is a wonderful thing to see a man born again—is their extreme simplicity.[102] Directly a man is really honest the miracle occurs. Many deceive themselves. They protest that they want to be rid of sin, and it isn't really true. Others do want to be rid of their sin, but selfishly, for their own ease, their own self-respect, or because they are afraid of being found out. Those find it difficult. But when a man hungers and thirsts to be rid of sin so that he may help others, it really is extraordinary how soon the step is taken from darkness to light, from sleep to waking. It seems natural and right, when one considers that the message of Jesus was unselfishness. There can't be any vital experience of religion where selfishness has got a hold, whatever form it takes.[103] What surprises one is not the miracle of conversion, but the ease with which even very good men will go on deceiving themselves all their life long; men who are moral and philanthropic, but with some root of selfishness in their hearts, which prevents them from ever experiencing a new birth or saving a man who is lost. Why do these people deceive themselves? It seems such a mad idea, attempting to hoodwink God. I suppose they are not properly awake, that they don't understand what they are doing."

Few of the followers of F.B. exercise so great an influence over

---

102 BB, pg. 62, "Most good ideas are simple, and this concept was the keystone of the new and triumphant arch through which we passed to freedom."
103 BB, pg. 93, "To be vital, faith must be accompanied by self sacrifice and unselfish, constructive action."

others as this gracious person whose voice and smile, could I convey them to this "brutish paper," would endear him to the reader and give a deeper meaning to his words.

I spoke to him a little of theological difficulties. He admitted those difficulties, and agreed that they will have to be faced; but he said, very modestly and unpretentiously, that redemption would remain the central truth of religious life whatever might be the future language of theology.

"There is no fact so great in the experience of men," he said quietly, "as the fact that a soul on the extreme edge of destruction can be redeemed to life merely by turning round—sincerely turning right round."[104]

The most beautiful of all the parables certainly teaches that the Father can do nothing until the son has turned his face homewards.

---

104 BB, pg. 25, "The great fact is just this, and nothing less: That we have had deep and effective spiritual experiences which have revolutionized our whole attitude toward life, toward our fellows and toward God's universe." And pg. 164, "See to it that your relationship with Him is right, and great events will come to pass for you and countless others. This is the Great Fact for us."

CHAPTER VI

BEAU IDEAL

CONSPICUOUS in the house-party for his good looks was a man well known at Eton and Oxford, whom we will here call Beau Ideal. Over six feet, with a fresh boyish complexion, clear bright eyes, thick fair hair very carefully brushed, a clipped moustache, and something a little dandiacal about his clothes, this young Hercules of twenty-four English summers looked exactly like the circulating library's idea of an officer in the Brigade of Guards.

I noticed that while he lounged in a deep chair, speaking with a tired drawl, as though discussion bored him, he was activity itself when he got upon his feet. One caught sight of him at times in voluminous flannels and coarse-knitted sweater hurrying away to get an hour's tennis; or missed him from the luncheon table to learn that he had gone off to play in a cricket match. Sometimes it seemed to me that behind his boyish handsomeness there smouldered the flames of a once difficult temper. But the chief impression he made on one's mind was that of the perfectly healthy, sport-loving, and well-bred young Briton at his topmost best. Whether he had brains was another matter. How he came to be interested in religion puzzled me a good deal.

He amused me one night by an answer he made to a challenging question by F.B. The Surgeon of Souls had been contrasting, with a deep and rather reproachful seriousness, the way in which the movement for personal religion was spreading in the Universities of the United States with that movement in the British Isles. He said it was up to English Varsity men to see that much more energy was put into this work; what did they propose to do about it? (Silence.) What suggestions had they to make? (Silence.) Surely some of them had at least a part of an idea in their minds.

After some slow-dragging moments of nervous silence, Beau Ideal, sprawling in a big chair, lazily made answer, "If you told Oxford men that an Oxford man wanted to talk to them about religion they wouldn't pay the smallest attention to you, beyond a glance to see if you were drunk or off your head. But I believe there is another University in England; if I remember rightly, at a place called Cambridge; and I rather think that if you told Oxford men a fellow from this extraordinary place wanted to speak to them they'd go, even if it was to hear about religion, just out of curiosity to see what manner of animal Cambridge produces."

In this way, rousing the Cambridge men of the party to intellectual reprisals, Beau Ideal made a valuable contribution to the debate. Behind the persiflage was an idea, and within the irony a truth.

Seldom have I been more out of my reckoning with a human being than I presently found myself in the case of this handsome young giant. He came to see me in London, and alone together I discovered that he was not merely interested in religion as a possible theory of existence, but that he was truly consumed with a fervorous passion for all those intellectual and moral sacrifices which orthodox religion so obviously calls upon a man to make. Instead of a dandy I had caught a fanatic.

His manner completely changed. There was the same lounging disposition of the big body, but no drawl in the speech, no sleepy languor of the eyelids. Indeed, there were moments when quite visibly he became electric, and had to put restraint on his enthusiasm; moments when his quick and eager words broke suddenly down, and a blush of misgiving came into his face, a look of inquiry darting from his eyes, as though the mind would discover whether it was not prejudicing its case by moral emotionalism. Wonderful to relate, Beau Ideal is a genuine firebrand.

From boyhood, I learned, he has had the greatest difficulty in bridling a hot temper. The sound of a voice could irritate him, an ugly fashion in clothes make him hate the wearer, an opinion with which he did not agree rouse in him an impulse almost homicidal. He has tramped many miles over the highlands merely to escape from people. He has sailed and fished for days only as an excuse to flee from society that rubbed him the wrong way. Games, which he plays with tremendous vigour, were the chief outlet in his boyhood for irritable energies boiling up within him to the fever point of exasperation.

When he went to Christ Church he was still first and foremost an athlete, but there was a disposition in him to scholarship, and he was soon regarded as an undergraduate with an intellectual future. He found the tentative, superior, and philosophical temperament of Oxford entirely to his liking. His set in the House was the best of its time. It was composed of men who took themselves seriously, but were careful not to let it be thought that they took themselves too seriously. In this set Beau Ideal, by grace of body and charm of mind, was a figure of some eminence.

His thoughts were occupied chiefly by politics and philosophy. He contracted an interest for social problems. The world appeared to him as a diverting problem providing endless opportunities for delightful theories—a serious problem, but a problem all the better for being regarded with a certain irony of outlook.

Across this intellectual life ran the interrupting diagonal of a sex pride. He knew very well that he was a rather out-of-the-way good-looking person. He liked to notice the effect he produced on entering a ballroom. It pleased him immensely that the prettiest girls, wherever he went, gave him special glances and wanted him very much to dance with them. He showed no outward sign of this pardonable vanity; indeed, he assumed an intentional modesty to aggravate the effect of his charm; but inwardly he was about as full of foppish conceit as any "lady's man" that ever lived.

So his days were passing, not innocent of feverish sin, but chiefly taken up with philosophy, games, dancing, and affairs of the wardrobe, when one summer's night he was introduced to F. B. in Peck Quad. F. B. suggested that they should take a walk round the Quad, and began to ask Beau Ideal what he was thinking about. Beau Ideal, rather puzzled by this direct invasion of his privacies, but setting it down to the crudeness of Yankee manners, began to speak about life in general—his interest in eugenics, birth control, the problems of population, and the chief social difficulties of the time.

All of a sudden F.B. said to him: "Those things aren't disturbing you. You know what's robbing you of peace, don't you?" And, then and there, as Beau Ideal puts it, he began "stirring up the mud."

It was a beautiful, still summer night, with pale stars above the roofs of the college, the moon coming up in a mist of silver, the sound of the ancient city at that late hour little more than a far-distant sea-murmur. Beau Ideal could hear his heart beating as he listened to the trenchant words of this inexplicable man walking at his side; he could feel his cheeks colouring in the cool air as the mud stirred up by the American got into the circulation of his blood and mounted to his conscience. Never before had a man spoken to him as this man was now speaking.

Left to himself, with a disturbed consciousness and a guilty conscience, Beau Ideal tried in vain to take up the threads of his former life. F.B. had said something to him which made the fact of sin a towering and menacing fact of human life. He could not escape from the thought that all the social and political problems with which he had hitherto amused his intellect—problems convenient enough as topics of conversation—were so many molehills in comparison with this single mountainous fact of human sin.

Discussions with some of his friends who had gone rather deeper into this same great matter with the American Surgeon of Souls presently led Beau Ideal to lend the light of his countenance to the proceedings of the Christian Student Movement in Christ Church. If you can imagine Apollo stepping down from Olympus to help an infant class to appreciate the poetry of Mrs. Hemans[105] or Martin Tupper[106] you may suitably figure to yourself the attitude of Beau Ideal in his association with the Christian Student Movement's activities at the House.

---

105 Felicia Hemans (1793-1835) was a popular English poet, the leading female poet of her time period.
106 Martin Tupper (1801-1889) was an English poet and novelist, and was a candidate for Poet Laureate, but lost to Tennyson.

He was careful from the first to make it understood that his interest in that movement was social and political. Where that movement was concerned with issues worthy the attention of an intellectual man of the world, there our young god was willing to appear in the Roman garments of a Mecænas.[107] As to anything so contrary to the established customs of good breeding as personal discussions concerning the hypothetical relations of an unproved soul with a theoretical God, clearly in that respect nothing could be expected of him.

But F.B. had stirred up the mud so effectually that when he was alone by himself Beau Ideal was far too conscious of his own personal sins—not other people's sins—for peace of mind. Instead of the boyish irritability which had once made such a turmoil of his days he found himself now assailed by a profound and morbid unrest of soul which robbed him of peace and dogged every step of his happiness.

To be rid of such a tax on his patience he played games harder than ever, and harder than ever applied himself to a study of philosophy. It seemed to him that with a healthy mind in a healthy body he would presently be able not only to form a satisfactory thesis of existence, but to get rid of certain bad habits which he did not doubt degraded him.

But the unrest continued. It continued till he found himself confronted by a choice, which he calls the choice between philosophy or religion. Either he had to remain outside the struggle of man's soul, looking on at it with interest, patience, tolerance, and a calming irony, or he had to take a plunge into a quite other fount and cleanse himself of that which fouled him, body and soul.

All his inclinations were towards philosophy; all his heredity was against religion.[108]

In this frame of mind he went away to Sark,[109] on purpose to

107 Gaius Mecænas (68 BC – 8 BC) was the wealthy patron of many Roman poets, including Virgil and Horace. He refused to join the Roman Senate, but was an advisor and friend to Emperor Augustus.
108 BB, pg. 44, "If a mere code of morals or a better philosophy of life were sufficient to overcome alcoholism, many of us would have recovered long ago."
109 Sark is a channel island, west of Guernsey, about 2 miles wide.

fight the matter out with himself and by himself. It happened that one day, sitting on a rock in a high wind, with a great and staggering sea breaking in vast commotion against that ironbound coast, so that he was drenched with spindrift and swayed by the gale, this problem resolved itself into one clear question which thus presented itself to his mind:

Is it true, or untrue, that philosophy, regarded as a mathematical system of thought, fails to provide an adequate answer to the question propounded by a system within it, namely ethics, as to *how* a man is to live according to his highest lights—or, as Aristotle would say, κατα τον ορθον λογον, according to right reason?[110]

He began his answer by confessing that a man does not need philosophy to teach him what is right and what is wrong. Philosophy is unnecessary to tell a man what he should do in the sphere of conduct. Within the man himself, born with him into this world, an inherent part of his nature, perhaps as old as the first movement of evolution, is a disposition towards his best, at any rate a recognition that there is a best and that there is a worst.

Then he saw that human progress—that is to say, human happiness and human freedom—had chiefly depended on man's response to this movement within him—this movement in the direction of the best which had so often in the history of humanity involved the supreme sacrifice.[111]

At this point he asked himself what part philosophy had played in that struggle. Many great philosophers had elevated man to a noble dignity by the exercise of purely rational faculties, but what part had philosophy itself played in freeing the multitude from the tyranny of evil habits and ennobling the moral character of the human race?

His own experience told him that philosophy is often employed to blind men's eyes to the real issues, to find an excuse for

110 κατα τον ορθον λογον (kata ton orthon logon,) 'According to right reason' a phrase from Aristotle's *Nicomachean Ethics*, but one that seems to have become a common usage among the later Stoics.
111 BB, pg. 93, "For if an alcoholic failed to perfect and enlarge his spiritual life through work and self-sacrifice for others, he could not survive the certain trials and low spots ahead." Cf. also pg. xxx, pg. 14-15.

delinquency, to explain away a cancer of moral life, to justify in theory practices which the conscience of the individual tells him to be wrong. The moral life of Plato[112]—who cares to think about it? Acton's[113] intellectual contempt for those who would find in climate or in chronology an excuse for evil—how justifiable! Plausible explanations, how often is this the work of philosophy in action!

Another idea presented itself to his mind. Philosophy gives man a false notion of liberty by challenging all rules and refusing to recognise the authority of, or the reverence due to, anything which is not explicable to the contemporary reason. It destroys all standards save those of its own time and its own creation. It is the declared enemy of humble faith. It will not take for granted even the most sacred intuitions of the human soul. It is incompatible with earnest moral endeavour.[114] In nearly all its aspects it is destructive and negative.

Such, he tells me, were the thoughts thrown up by the ocean under the stern cliffs of Sark—thoughts no less numerous, troubled and jumbled than the waves of that disordered sea.

The battle, of course, was only half fought. He was left merely with the ruins of a boy's faith in philosophy as a breakwater against humanity's sea of troubles.

"It is the prerogative of youth, I suppose," he wrote to me of that time, "to rail against things as they are, and in those days I shared keenly in that dissatisfaction, and included myself among the least satisfactory phenomena. The failure of materialism came to me as a profound[115] conviction; and, against that, the necessity

---

112 Perhaps he is referring to the fact that Plato had a mistress, Archeanassa. Or that he wrote love poems in his youth addressed to men. Or that in his political life he flirted with joining the Thirty Tyrants, before they prosecuted Socrates. Or that he got entangled with Dionysus, the tyrant of Syracuse.

113 Lord Acton (1834-1902) wrote much against the dangers of power. His phrase, "absolute power corrupts absolutely," is well known today.

114 BB, pg. 46, "To us, the Realm of Spirit is broad, roomy, all inclusive; never exclusive or forbidding to those who earnestly seek."

115 BB, pg. 14, "God comes to most men gradually, but His impact on me was sudden and profound." Cf. Also, the Second Appendix on Spiritual Experience, pg. 567, "He finally realizes that he has undergone a profound alteration in his reaction

to make use of spiritual force. It became clear that the only ultimate significance in life was genuine moral effort. I suppose the
appeal came most directly as a question of the general welfare and
happiness of people. They themselves had failed to promote their
own welfare. What must be done?"

A little later he was able to say: "Even the most superficial
study of the Christian religion was enough to show me that in
the sophisticated atmosphere of modern times, in a welter of sex
psychology and necromancy of nearly every kind, an age of few
restraints and no reverences, an age with no holy of holies for 'the
unsanctified curiosities of common men,' the simple ethic of Jesus
would work a healthy change. Honesty in commerce, sincerity in
the Church, sympathy between employer and employed, purity
and decency in social life, idealism and earnestness in political
life—what a change would such things effect! *Pari passu* with
these things came the challenge of one's own conscience—the
searching thought of one's own personal morality. I heard a friend
say of Dr. Arnold of Rugby, 'He was old fashioned; he believed in
God.' That set me thinking. I thought to myself, How much better
it would be for the world if more people believed in God. I got so
far as to acknowledge that for myself, if I were not to be disloyal
to conscience, it was essential for me to believe in God."

Thus matters stood with him when he was invited to the
house party at Cambridge of which mention has been made in
the chapter called "A Rugger Blue." Desire to see more of F.B., a
feeling in his own mind that something more was yet demanded
of him than an intellectual acknowledgment of the ethical value of
Christianity, made him accept this invitation.

He says that he learned during those wonderful days in Cambridge the way of believing in God. The word *spiritual* as applied
to a human being, he came to see, implied a person through whom
the divine spirit could work. He began from that point to understand what he calls "the intimate working of the philosophy of
Jesus." Before he could reasonably hope to be in some communion
with the divine spirit, manifestly he must attune his moral being
to that celestial tone. His particular need, he felt, was for honesty,

to life; that such a change could hardly have been brought about by himself alone."

first with himself and then with others; a genuine willingness to share burdens and difficulties; a disposition to pray readily and continually, out of a sense of great need and inexpressible unworthiness; an increasing consideration for the feelings of other people, taking into account their desires, their needs, and their limitations; finally, a complete submission of himself to the supreme ideal of human life, Christ Jesus, with an instant and rejoicing readiness to make any sacrifice of himself and his fortunes at the call of the least of those whom he could help.[116]

There came a moment at that house party when he made this submission of his will to the Will of God, when he decided that henceforth he would live in absolute singleness of mind, with no thought of self, with everything he had or possessed at the service of his Master, his soul hungering and thirsting for the perfection of God.

In one of his letters to me, written before an even greater experience of spiritual power, he said: "There is much more I might say, but this will be enough just now. At every point we are called upon for sober thinking, and for discipline and for earnestness. The further I go the more profoundly am I impressed with the significance of *simplicity*. All the greatest ideas and truths in the world are simple. The Bible is simple. The highest prayer one can make or know of is the simplest of all.[117] The issues of morality are simple—purity, honesty, sincerity, discipline. Jesus led a simple life in a humble station. The argument *ex contrarie* (i.e. that that which is not simple is probably unsound) applies forcibly to ever so many things, e.g. philosophy, if not to everything. Comparisons are odious, but we learn in time to rely on some ultimate criterion."

Since those words were written he has paid a visit to the United States in company with F.B., and from F.B. and others I learn that he has exercised a very powerful influence among American undergraduates. I do not wonder, for he is a singularly taking person. Moreover, his spiritual growth is visible to the eyes of all

---

116 BB, Second Appendix, pg. 568, "Willingness, honesty, and open-mindedness are the essentials of recovery. But these are indispensable."
117 BB, pg. 62, "Most good ideas are simple, and this concept was the keystone of the new and triumphant arch through which we passed to freedom."

his friends. One of them described to me that growth[118] as "tremendous," adding that Beau Ideal had gone in for "a most severe self-discipline," that he had "absolutely given up no end of things," that he was now "completely in the saddle," and that he allows "nothing to stand in the way of helping other men." All this I can well believe. The fire was there from the first. Such men, however long they may hold back from the dreadful moment of an absolute decision, will go to the uttermost extreme of self-sacrifice when once they have escaped from the former things of their tyranny.

It may be interesting to glance for a moment at the intellectual characteristics of his faith. He finds no difficulty in thinking of Jesus as "the propitiation for the sins of the whole world." He finds the greatest help in thinking of Jesus as the one power by whom men come to God and as the one being before whom we could not do a shameful act. He is convinced that the Bible and prayer are essential to spiritual life. In his last letter written from America he tells me that he is entering with others into "A First Century Christian Fellowship," explaining that they wish to get back to the type of Christianity which was maintained by the Apostles— "We not only accept their beliefs, but are also decided to practice their methods."

He announces in detail the elemental beliefs of a First Century Christianity. He believes in:

The possibility of immediate and continued fellowship with the Holy Spirit—guidance.

The proclamation of a redemptive gospel—personal, social, and national salvation.

The possession of fullness of life—rebirth, and an ever-increasing power and wisdom.

The propagation of their life by individuals to individuals—personal religion.

Out of these beliefs proceeds the method of propagation:

118 BB, pg. 66, "But with the alcoholic, whose hope is the maintenance and growth of a spiritual experience, this business of resentment is infinitely grave." Cf. pg. 12, 47, 117.

Love for the sinner.

Hatred of the sin.

Fearless dealing with sin.

The presentation of Christ as the cure for sin.

The sharing and giving of self, with and for others.

"We are more concerned," he writes, "with testifying to real experiences, explicable only on the hypothesis that God's power has brought them to pass, through Christ, than with teaching an abstract ethical doctrine."

From this it will be seen that there is a tendency in his mind not only to make large assumptions (that is characteristic of all practical people), but also perhaps to regard obstinate credulity as a virtue. He seems ready to take over from one particular version of the First Century any phrase or idea which that version associates with the apostles—not to take it over as poetry, or as an attempt of the Eastern mind to utter inexpressible mystery in the language of metaphor, but as an axiom in a mathematical system of thought.

I remember that in one of his former letters, speaking of the commending simplicity of the Christian religion, he remarks that the question of Jesus, *What think ye of Christ?* is simplicity itself.[119] One is obliged to say that it is quite impossible for a man who has made even a cursory study of the documents to believe that Jesus ever asked such a question; certainly it was never asked in that form. The word Christ was not known to Jesus, and was never applied by the Greeks to any human being until after His death. Again, it is a solitary question, remote from the whole character of the life of Jesus; a life, we may surely say, which never wasted

---

119 Matthew 22:41-46 KJV. "41 While the Pharisees were assembled, Jesus questioned them: 42 "What do you think about the Christ? Whose son is He?" "David's," they answered. 43 Jesus said to them, "How then does David in the Spirit call Him 'Lord'? For he says: 44 'The Lord said to my Lord, "Sit at My right hand until I put Your enemies under Your feet."' 45 So if David calls Him 'Lord,' how can He be David's son?" 46 No one was able to answer a word, and from that day on no one dared to question Him any further.

a moment in metaphysical speculation. Not what a man thought about Him was the preoccupation of Jesus, but whether that man was doing the Will of God. "Suffer little children to come unto Me, and forbid them not; for of such is the Kingdom of Heaven."[120]

The danger of enthusiasm in religion is a very definite record of history; but if we go more deeply into that matter we shall surely find that this danger was only great and perilous to the progress of civilisation when it took the form of enthusiasm for a particular answer to the question, *What think ye of Christ?*

Enthusiasm for love, modesty, unselfish service, moral discipline, and spiritual excellence, and the character of Jesus, has contributed to the progress of civilisation nothing but good. A movement of personal religion in our own time may render priceless service to that difficult progress, and to all the most enduring of human interests; but one must doubt whether such a movement can ever emerge into the main current of existence if its little streams are dammed by theological tests.

I feel about Beau Ideal and those with whom he now appears to be associating himself that in their enthusiasm for the liberation and power of spiritual life they are somewhat dangerously disposed to regard theological objections to the Catholic religion as sins against the Holy Spirit, and to confuse an unquestioning credulity with the beautiful and ineffable virtue of aspiring faith.

It is natural, of course, for an impetuous and grateful mind, which has suffered sharply in the furnace of temptation, to regard with immeasurable gratitude the person who has opened to it the door of escape; but upon each of us, surely, is laid the obligation most seriously to ask himself whether one can ever be morally justified in taking over from another man, merely because he has helped us, a dogmatic theology (which we propose henceforth to make a religious test for those we would attempt to help) without a personal and very conscientious scrutiny.

---

120 Matthew 19:14.

CHAPTER VII

PRINCETON

THIS narrative illustrates one of those curious paradoxes which sooner or later confront every historian of religion who attempts to lay down hard and fast rules for spiritual experience.

It is the story of a changed life with no red-letter day in its calendar. One finds no moment in its progress where a definite break was made consciously with the past. It tells of no crisis of emotion setting a term to illusion and opening the gates to illumination. It is as true a document of conversion as any to be found in the pages of *The Varieties of Religious Experience*, and yet it seems to question the familiar saying of William James that "the crisis of self-surrender has always been, and must always be, regarded as the vital turning-point of the religious life."

Perhaps such a story may be helpful and encouraging to those who have grown in spiritual happiness just as they have grown in intellectual happiness; it will not, I hope, minister in any way to the moral indecision of those who, needing it so conspicuously, shrink from the apparent ordeal of self-surrender. For the majority of men, one suspects, the crisis is essential.[121]

Until he was twenty years of age this agreeable American, who is now only twenty-five, made no acquaintance with dogmatic theology. He grew up in a home which took religion for granted. His father, a man of wealth, was firmly religious in the moral sense of that word; a lawyer, and a prominent citizen of his state, he stood for "clean politics," for honest dealing in trade, and for the domestic virtues in family life. Both from this father and from his mother, who was also strongly religious in an ethical manner,

---

121 BB, pg. 53, " When we became alcoholics, crushed by a self-imposed crisis we could not postpone or evade, we had to fearlessly face the proposition that either God is everything or else He is nothing."

the boy learned to regard a lie as cowardly and shameful, and to feel that there was something superior and honourable in straightforwardness. The other member of the family was a sister, a little older than himself, very charming and sympathetic, of a natural refinement, and with an inclination to the deeper things of religious life.

The family was exclusive to an extreme degree. This exclusiveness was not dictated by social considerations, but by a love of privacy and quiet. The father was a cultivated man with a fine library. He loved reading, and found his chief intellectual happiness in history and biography. He encouraged his son to read the best order of books. "Never read trash," was one of his constant injunctions. He conveyed the impression that the mind could be soiled by contact with the second-rate.

There was no feeling for art in the family. Music had no place in it; painting awoke no interest. The happiness of the household was complete, and felt no need for these things. Discussion never occurred at the table. The mind of the family was agreed upon everything. Occasionally the father would speak with contempt of a shady politician, or express himself strongly on the behaviour of a statesman or a newspaper; but there was never anything in the nature of debate or discussion.

The son was sent to a Quaker school because it was the best in the town. Perhaps he acquired at that school something of the Quaker spirit. One sees in his handsome face a certain austerity of the spirit, and feels in his manner an almost preternatural gravity of mind. He is extraordinarily self-possessed, but without the least trace—on the contrary, indeed—of self-satisfaction or loudness of mind. The voice is low, the dark eyes are solemn, the expression of the face is impassive. He makes much the same impression on one, even in full daylight, as is made by a stranger speaking from the shadows of a large and curtained room which is lighted by a sleeping fire. It is as if he dwells far back in the recesses of his mind, so far back, at any rate, that the world can never steal his quiet or soil his peace.

At seventeen years of age he proceeded to Princeton University. There was no shock of any kind in this first acquaintance with the world. He was happy in making a friend of Richard Cleveland, son of President Cleveland, for this Richard was a social reformer very unlikely to get into wrong sets. The two young men regarded one aspect of Varsity life with great contempt. There are no colleges in Princeton; only dormitories. In order to get something of the feeling of college life, the undergraduates form clubs, chiefly for eating purposes, and these clubs divide themselves into clubs with luxurious buildings, suitable for the rich and the distinguished, and hugger-mugger clubs, suitable for the poor student.

Richard Cleveland and the man of whom I am writing regarded this state of things as vulgar and bad. Such a division, they said, set up false standards. The business of a University is to mix all sorts and conditions of men together; to unify, not to divide; certainly not to exalt wealth as something higher than genius or poverty. Moreover, a certain amount of drinking and gambling went on in the luxurious clubs; the moral influence was decidedly not good. Of one mind on this subject, and being prominent men in that year, they opposed themselves to the tradition. Out of a class of three hundred, they enlisted a hundred men who pledged themselves not to join the expensive and aristocratic clubs.

It must not be thought that this social activity created in the mind of our austere undergraduate a desire for public life. It is important to know that he remained aloof from personal friendships, and was intimate with no one. His influence was felt in the University with no exertion on his part. He found himself elected to offices he had never sought; before he quite realised what had happened he discovered himself in a position of some moral responsibility. Still, he remained the quiet, serious, self-contained, and reserved student, making no friends, seeking no acquaintances, inviting no confidences.

On his vacations he listened to his sister's account of religious activity at the college in which she was distinguishing herself. He was interested, felt that it was the right thing for her to be interested in such work, but there the matter ended.

When he returned to Princeton, he found himself directing

a movement half social and half religious—a movement to get University men interested in boys' clubs and summer camps. At one of these summer camps he made the acquaintance of a bright and intelligent newsboy, who began to talk to him more and more seriously about religion, until one day he suddenly blurted out a confession and asked his rich young friend for advice. The undergraduate recommended cold baths, no lounging about, brisk habits of mind and body. Some months afterwards the boy drew him on one side, and said that this plan did not work, asking if there was nothing else to be tried.

The fact that he really had nothing else to advise rather preyed on the undergraduate's mind. He began to pay some attention to the question of personal religion. He heard about the work which F.B. was doing in some of the Universities. Then he met F.B. and was invited to attend a little Retreat of men interested in personal religion. He was disappointed at first in F.B. A temperamental reticence held him back for some time from joining this Retreat. But in the end he was persuaded to go, and he went with a thoroughly uncomfortable feeling, convinced that he would be a fish out of water.

He said to me, "I have never had any moral struggle. I have never been aware of any problems in myself. I could always get along without outside help. Religion only interested me when I came to see how madly other men needed it to save themselves from going on the rocks. I learned as I went along that there are such things as temptations. Happily for me, I was altogether unaware of such temptations; my tastes, my temperament, my home-life, made certain things ugly and dislikable to me; but other men, I discovered, did not see those things in the same light. Among the men who went to F.B.'s Retreat were some whom I knew fairly well, and knew to be doing no good. I saw these men changed. It was the sudden and complete change in these men,[122] under F.B.'s influence, which made an effect upon my mind. It was impossible not to be impressed. I never tackled anyone my-

---

122 BB, pg. xxxi, "From a trembling, despairing, nervous wreck, had emerged a man brimming over with self-reliance and contentment. I talked with him for some time, but was not able to bring myself to feel that I had known him before." Cf. pg. 84, "Our whole attitude and outlook upon life will change."

self, and nobody tackled me; but I saw something of this tackling, and I saw quite clearly its extraordinary effect. Still I felt reluctant to take up any work of that nature. It was good for other men, but not for me. I had no bias that way, no gift for such work. My whole temperament was opposed to it."

Soon after this a youngish man came to the University as Secretary of the Christian Association. He had been changed by F.B. He talked to my friend, told him that he too had been just as repelled by F.B., and then proceeded to relate what F.B. had done for him. The happiness of this man, the tremendous drive of his personality, his reality, his conviction that men could be saved from sin by no other method, made a marked impression on my friend's mind.

Still, no decision was taken.

A little later there were religious conferences. F.B.'s spirit, he says, had prepared their atmosphere. It was a friendly, hopeful, and perfectly natural atmosphere. The absence of anything official or sacerdotal struck him agreeably. Men of all sorts were there—scholars and athletes—and all of them talked in their natural voices, wore ordinary clothes, and behaved as if they were debating a political question. He found himself growing more and more convinced that F.B. was right. He had no personal interview. He was simply one of a group. F.B.'s remarks were made to the whole group, never to him in particular. But gradually, profoundly, imperceptibly, the change was taking place.

Day by day he became more certain. Day by day he saw what he was going to do. There was no crisis; no moment in which he decided; no moment in which religion suddenly became real. Everything in the old life shaded off into the new life forming within him. God did not suddenly cease to be a name and suddenly become a Person. It was all like the coming of a dawn—a gradual emergence from darkness to twilight, from twilight to day.[123]

But the daylight was there, and he saw visibly what was before

---

123 BB, pg. 8 "How dark it is before the dawn!" According to the Joe and Charlie seminars on the Big Book, one of the titles they suggested for the book was "*Comes the Dawn.*"

him. An only son, very expensively educated, who goes to a proud father and announces that he wishes to devote his life to the poverty and service of religion cannot be sure of congratulation. But this announcement had to be made. So great now was the gradual and imperceptible change in his soul that he could contemplate no other life. To give all he possessed to the work of helping men was now his destiny.

"There was no real opposition in my family," he told me. "My sister was back in the home, engaged in religious work, and the atmosphere was perhaps changed by her work. In any case, my father was extremely kind and understanding. My mother expressed a strong feeling that the step I contemplated might not be wise, but she was quite affectionate. Everything seemed to be made easy for me. I took up the work, and I am happier than I have ever been before. It has opened to me a door to one of the greatest things in life—friendship."

He spoke of this great thing with his usual self-mastery, and yet it was impossible not to realise an enthusiasm in the measured words. He had no glowing language for the mystical experiences of the religious life, and no glowing words either for the wonderful delight of human friendship; but he spoke of this high human pleasure with a certain ring in his voice which I never caught when he was speaking of other subjects.

He said, "I had no idea that friendship was such a beautiful thing. I came late to it, because our family kept so much to itself, and because by nature I was very reserved as a boy. We never seemed to meet other people. Certainly I never played with other children. I met boys of my own age at school, but only at school; they never came back to our house. I never *knew* them. In a sense I had never known anybody at all. But this work of personal religion brings friendship into a man's life in its highest conceivable form. I am now so rich in friends that I smile when people speak to me of the self-sacrifice in religion. The life a man lays down in this matter is not a very desirable thing. The life he takes up again is full of the deepest possible happiness. One finds that it is very difficult to help another man until one really cares for him, and directly one cares for another man not only is it easy to help him, but you get this most beautiful thing of friendship—friendship that counts no cost in its longing to be of service. I doubt if many people who live entirely without religion have any idea of what friendship is—true human friendship."

He makes one think of Bacon's great saying, "*no man that imparteth his joys to his friend, but he joyeth the more; and no man that imparteth his griefs to his friend, but he grieveth the less.*"[124]

This work has not only brought him a pleasure of which he had no experience, but a new knowledge of which he had never dreamed.[125]

"I am astounded," he said to me, "by the moral chaos in men's lives. Difficulties about which I knew nothing present themselves now at every turn. Sin, I discover, plays an unimaginably great part in human life. Men who might be of service to a nation, and who might enjoy peace of mind and a life of the highest happiness, are frustrated by inclinations which they find themselves powerless to resist, even when they see clearly that they are disastrous. I used to think that a man went to the bad because he liked going to the bad. It always seemed to me that men who did things which most decent men regard as unworthy or even contemptible, did those things because they found pleasure in them. Now I know that many of these men, at any rate at the beginning of their careers, do these things against their own judgment, even against their own will. Something within them drives them on. They are suddenly attacked by irresistible power. They describe themselves as being forced, driven, or hurled into ways which they hate. All this was at one time quite unintelligible to me. I never realised that there is a struggle in the soul. Now I know that any man whose personality is divided must always live at the sport of treacherous inclinations."

He also said to me: "I do not at all think that sex difficulties are the chief battle-ground of youth. I regard those difficulties as

---

124 Francis Bacon (1561-1626) was a statesman who served King James I as Lord Chancellor and Attorney General. He was a polymath who wrote widely on science, philosophy, and religion.
125 BB, pg. 25, "We have found much of heaven and we have been rocketed into a fourth dimension of existence of which we had not even dreamed."

much the same as lethargy, pride, idleness, coldness, meanness, selfishness. It is even harder sometimes to break down a man's conceit or selfishness than to strengthen another man against sensual weakness. All sin has its roots in selfishness.[126] Chaos is inseparable from selfishness."

He spoke to me also of his view concerning the future of religion in the struggle of man's soul.

"I have learned," he said, "from this work of personal religion to distrust organisation and to see a quite extraordinary power in the leaven of personality. No doubt organisation of some kind will long continue, and will be useful; but I feel confident that the future belongs to personal religion, by which I mean the unofficial, the unprofessional, and the uninstitutional influence of one man on another.[127] I am quite sure humanity must be saved man by man, not in droves and herds. I doubt if anyone can profoundly help another until he cares for him as a friend. And until intercourse is absolutely intimate how can one soul understand another soul—understand it in such a manner as to render help?"

He told me of the change which is now going on in the Universities of America. There is a new seriousness among undergraduates, an increasing sense of responsibility, a visible movement towards spiritual life. All this is entirely due to personal religion. It is the work of a few men like F.B. It has received no impetus from official quarters. Swiftly, as if some mysterious power were at work, the spirit spreads from University to University, and religion becomes a real thing, a thing of infinite moment to the individual, of enormous importance to the future of the human race.

Directly, he says, a man feels that religion is a real power in human life, not merely a subject for theological discussion, he becomes interested in it. And directly he discovers that it can work a miracle in his own soul he seeks to understand it. A few men with this wonderful leaven of personality could change the world.

---

126 BB, pg. 62, "Selfishness—self-centeredness! That, we think, is the root of our troubles."

127 BB, pg. 18, "But the ex-problem drinker who has found this solution, who is properly armed with facts about himself, can generally win the entire confidence of another alcoholic in a few hours."

CHAPTER VIII

A YOUNG SOLDIER

ONE of the guests at the house-party to which I referred in my introduction was pointed out to me as a man who had distinguished himself in the war by notable courage. He looked a mere boy—one of those freshskinned, fair-haired, urchin-like striplings whose faces flush with a grinning self-consciousness when they find themselves objects of observation.

He was tall and slight, with an inclination to stoop his head. But for the sadness of his voice, which is rather deep in note, and the gravity of his words in discussion, one would think of him as a sly schoolboy always on the alert to pull somebody's leg or to work off a pun. So much suppressed laughter, so much restrained gaiety, so much controlled roguishness, it would be difficult to find in the face of the most frivolous-minded tormentor of a schoolmaster. It was difficult for me to think of this jolly-looking youth as a soldier; more difficult to believe that he had passed through a religious crisis.

He told me that his father, who was a well-known man in English public life, died when he was eight years of age. "Yet," he said, "my impression of him is quite clear; his personality was unforgettable." As for his mother, who is still alive, he declared that she is a mother beyond all praise.

In a home so enviable as this, with one brother as a companion, M. grew up to boyhood, not merely shielded from all coarse influences which might throw miserable shadows across the radiance of a child's natural innocence, but encouraged to find his highest delight in occupations wholesome both for mind and body. The books he read were calculated to develop refinement of spirit; the games he played were calculated to develop his courage and his muscles. When he went to a preparatory school he was as good a specimen[128] of healthy, hearty, clean-minded, and intelligent English boyhood as any father could wish to see.

Unhappily for his development, there was a master at this school who was tormented by a devil of lust, and whose evil and furtive spirit corrupted the whole school. The boy learned vice at the hands of one who was paid to teach him virtue. He appears to have slipped into bad habits, as so many small boys do, with no apprehension at all of their consequences, physical or moral. Nevertheless he was not without knowledge that what he did was wrong, that it was something to be done out of sight, that it was an act of which he felt ashamed. It was with a feeling of relief that he found himself in a public school, where the moral tone was healthier and where he came under the stimulating influences of "some ripping masters."

Dogged by the vice he had learned at his first school, M. made a gallant fight for his self-respect, and gradually obtained a fair mastery over dangerous dispositions. He did well in games and well in school. He began to enjoy himself with the happiness of one who feels that things are straightening out, that the path before him leads to success, and that success can be gained with comparative ease. He won a scholarship for Oxford, and went up to the University with an appetite for all the best things which life offers at its charming threshold to the happiest order of manhood—that order of manhood which finds as superlative a pleasure in the acquisition of knowledge as in an increasing skill in difficult games.

One term of great happiness passed away, and then came the European war, claiming him as a soldier of England. From others I learn that he rose quickly to the rank of captain, that he was distinguished throughout his service for an unquailing courage and a singularly gentle regard for the welfare of his men, and that he won enviable distinctions in the great Battle of the Somme, falling at last to an attack of poison-gas.

When he recovered from this rather desperate affliction he was sent back to Oxford. The war had weakened in him his enthu-

128 BB, pg. xxxii, "I see him now and then and he is as fine a specimen of manhood as one could wish to meet."

siasm for scholarship, and had heightened in him his passion for games. He found an extraordinary delight in physical fitness. As if war had whetted his appetite for danger, he loved chiefly those games which involved risk of limb. When he could not play such games he rode about the country on a motorcycle, loving speed for itself and almost seeking those "narrow squeaks" which make the elderly spectator hold his breath.

It was in the rush of this athletic period, when his body was at its fittest and his mind freest from anxiety, that sexual trouble began once more to invade. But Oxford provided for him at this time something of an aid in his distress. He discovered the pleasure of friendship. There were rooms in which he was always welcome; there were delightful men always willing to talk. Among these men it was natural to discuss religion, and religion came back to his mind, consecrated by the memory of his father, and sacred with the thought of his mother, to help him in the loneliness of his conflict. But the stir of sex in his blood was not to be stilled, and though he might again and again overthrow that powerful motion in his whole being, yet the thing was there, haunting him, irking him, gnawing at his self-respect, shadowing his natural happiness.

In one of his discussions with a friend he heard for the first time of F.B., and was curious rather than interested by what he heard. At any rate he made no effort to see F.B., and continued to fight his battle in his own way. Soon after this he was badly broken in a Rugger smash, and was carted off to hospital with more injuries to his bones than the Great War had been able to inflict.

One day, lying in his bed at this hospital, a stranger came to see him. It was F.B. F.B. had been told by one of M.'s friends that there was a man in hospital who might be glad, he rather thought, to have a talk with him. Accordingly F.B., brisk, smiling, and quietly cheerful, presented himself at the bedside of football's victim.

"He made no impression upon me," said M., "neither one way nor the other. It never occurred to me to think of him as an out-of-the-way sort of person. He seemed perfectly natural, not particularly interesting, and certainly not in the least striking. But after he had left me I was conscious of a very curious feeling about him. I wanted to see him again. It wasn't a case of wanting to see a person one likes, or a person who has interested one by his ideas, but wanting to see a man who had made no other impression except this curious and inexplicable impression that one did very much want to see him again."

The next time F.B. came to M.'s bedside he made another impression. He was still an average person, still a person who was not in the least dramatic or even notable, yet he left behind him in M.'s mind the distinct sensation that he could help him. "I couldn't explain to myself why I had this feeling," M. told me; "I tried to reason the thing out, but couldn't see the ghost of an explanation. We had said nothing of a serious nature. There was no sense of intimacy. I was still conscious of his difference as a Yankee. And yet there it was; I could not shake out of my mind the notion that this unremarkable man could help me to straighten things out as no other man had yet done."

F.B.'s account of the matter is as follows: "One of his friends had spoken to me about him. He mentioned no trouble, but said that M. was a man he'd like me to meet. He spoke of his services in the war, told me about his fame as a Rugger player, said he was altogether a very fine fellow, and then mentioned that he was lying in the hospital, cracked up pretty badly. I knew I had to see this man. I knew, too, directly I saw him what his trouble was. We talked of just ordinary things. I didn't bother to know whether he liked me or not; all I knew was that for certain he would one day ask me to help him.

"That day came. He didn't find it easy to tell me the whole story. He got as far, with great difficulty, as telling me that he wasn't as happy as he wanted to be, and that he thought I might possibly be able to help him. I helped him right there, at that very moment. I helped him by telling him what his trouble was. It hit him like a blow from a hammer. After that it was easy for him, easy for me, easy for God. He's one of the finest fellows living, brave as a lion, yet shy as a girl. A beautiful nature—a real man with all the delicacy of a woman.

"Directly the trouble was out in the open he really hated it. With this hatred was a longing for all that a good man means by the Name of God. There was no wrestle, no struggle. He came to himself in a moment. Already he has done remarkable work, and when he has taken his degree as a doctor he will use his life entirely for God."

M. tells me that one of the greatest things F.B. did for him was freeing his mind for discussing this moral trouble with other men. An enormous change came into his life directly the sense of secret shame was dissipated. The evil lost its power. He found himself possessed of an altogether new strength. He was conscious of an altogether new liberty.[129]

To complete the happiness of his freedom from a noxious obsession he found that he could help other men to get their various temptations into the open, and that once in the open it was easy for them—most of them, at any rate—to realise the need for hating their sins before they could expect answers to their prayers.

I asked him to tell me what his opinion was of the morals of men at the Universities. He replied that, so far as his experience went, the present generation of young men is a healthy one. There is no "smuttiness" among them. The vast majority want to conquer their bad habits. It would be a very gross perversion of the truth to think of these young men as accepting vice as the natural order of things. They don't narrate their adventures. They don't compare their experiences. They don't talk about these matters; certainly those who do don't talk flippantly. There is a terrible struggle going on. It is a silent struggle. There are many defeats in that struggle, but no surrender on the part of the average man. Sport helps them more than orthodox religion, for orthodox religion seems to ignore this tremendous battlefield of youth; at any rate, it has nothing to offer which is recognised by the fighters as a help. What does help, what does enable most men to get the victory, is the personal religion inculcated by F.B. And there is far more of this work going on than the dons know. It is a part of the friend-

---

129 BB, pg. 75, "Once we have taken this step, withholding nothing, we are delighted. We can look the world in the eye. We can be alone at perfect peace and ease. Our fears fall from us. We begin to feel the nearness of our Creator."

ship of University life, widening its influence with every term.

One of the stories he told me, very modestly, of his own efforts to help other men is well worth telling here. In none of these stories (need I assert it of so gallant and gentle a man?) was there the least suggestion of exalting his own power over other lives. His sole object in telling them was to show me how the drive of sympathy can help a man who rather shrinks from such work to change the lives of others. His great contention is that F.B. has discovered for him the central truth of spiritual life, the pearl of great price, and that this truth is destined to save the soul of the world. He is quite sure about that. The soul can definitely deal direct with God.[130]

Among his fellow medical students he came across a man who had been with him at his public school. They renewed the friendship of those days, found that they had been fighting together in France without knowing it, and gradually entered into an intimate relationship.

This friend of schooldays told M. that when he went out to France he was engaged to be married. The brutality of the war atmosphere, with its manifold depressions and its inescapable temptations, preyed upon his moral energy, chafing him, but could not impair his loyalty to the girl in England. For two years of constant danger and surrounding bestiality he kept faith with idealism. He was as true as steel. Then he returned from the war to find that this girl had formed another attachment and wished to throw him over.

In the bitterness of his grief and the irony of his disillusion he went to the dogs. Alone in London, hating his solitude, longing for sympathy, and tortured by the thought that he had been true to a woman in vain, he sought to forget his troubles in the society of harlots.[131] Revulsion overcame him after every one of these visits, a revulsion bitter as gall, but again and again he went back, driven by an intolerable sense of loneliness. "Many men," he told

---

130 BB, pg. 46, "We found that God does not make too hard terms with those who seek Him."
131 BB, pg. 56, "Post-war disillusionment, ever more serious alcoholism, impending mental and physical collapse, brought him to the point of self-destruction."

M., "go to these poor girls simply for companionship. They are the kindest people in London to the friendless man eating his heart out in lodgings."

The manner in which M. has been able to help this particular person is simply by giving him a sense of loyalty to his own higher nature and by providing him with an altogether more abiding companionship. But the bitterness of the man's heart is not yet wholly gone, and the sense of the divine companionship is not yet firmly established. Still is he overtaken from time to time by an unbearable feeling of solitude and forlornness; but now, instead of seeking a cure for that ill where no cure is to be found, he comes to M., and to M. confesses his feebleness. "We are helping each other," is M.'s account of the matter.

No man could be freer than M. from that insufferable arrogance, or self-satisfaction, which disfigures so many people who feel themselves to be called by God to the service of converting other men. He speaks with quiet reverence, but an extreme diffidence, of his belief that his power to help other men is increasing,[132] and he looks forward to the day when as a doctor in some foreign Christian mission he may be able to exert that power with far greater effect. The power is there. He has no doubt about that. The ability to use it must be determined by his own response to its unaltering conditions.

He seems to me to be studying the laws of the spiritual world as the man of science studies the laws of the physical world. He is rightly making experiments with his soul. But below the inquiring mind is a spirit which believes unquestionably and with deep gladness in the existence of a God who is desirous of communicating Himself to His creature; and in the mind itself, that mind which inquires and investigates, is the clear knowledge that hatred of sin, and a clean bill from all forms of selfishness, must go before that craving desire for moral wisdom which establishes connection with the Eternal Righteousness. He does not announce himself as a discoverer, but he is certainly a traveller.

---

132 BB, pg. 84, "We vigorously commenced this way of living as we cleaned up the past. We have entered the world of the Spirit. Our next function is to grow in understanding and effectiveness."

The moral and spiritual differences separating such men as this charming young person from the offensive type of evangelical who went about in the eighties asking everyone whom he encountered, "Are you saved?" seem to me as great as the moral and spiritual differences which separate the writings of Plato from the writings of Ibsen, or the life of John Hampden from the life of Rousseau.[133] It is an entirely new type. It is a phenomenon in religious experience. With all the earnestness and unflinching realism of the older type of evangelicalism there is a delicacy, a modesty, a sweetness, and a tolerance in this new protagonist of personal religion which renders him, I think, a force of great hope for the future.

---

133 We presume the reader knows the difference between Plato and Henrik Ibsen. However, John Hampden (1595-1643) was a lesser known figure, who fought for Parliament against the Crown in the lead up to the English Civil War. He was an effective leader and organizer, and the Founding Father's used his name as an example to justify their own American Revolution. Later on, he was appropriated by British radicals who created "Hampden Clubs" to use his name to petition for reform in Great Britain. Contract with Jean-Jacques Rousseau (1712-1778), who was a philosopher and radical who advocated against private property, against civilization itself with his idea of the Noble Savage, and who courted political outrage at almost every turn, and led a very disordered personal life

CHAPTER IX
THE VIRGINIAN

HERE, to wind up these brief narratives, is the story of a blithe and hard-hitting spirit whose blood may well have descended to him from those Englishmen, "the flower and force of a kingdom," as Sir John Smyth described them to Lord Burghley in the sixteenth century, who then fought in Flanders and who "went voluntary to serve of a gaiety and joyalty of mind."[134]

The vigour of the man, the sheer delight he gets out of his struggle, the uncompromising character of his attack, and the warm friendliness of his nature, should bring him close enough to the people in England who still acknowledge the ancient tradition of Elizabethan adventure. The phrase used of F.W. Robertson may well be used of him. He is a *troubadour* of God.[135]

He was born in a fox-hunting country, beautiful with the softness and tenderness of our English shires, with far views from the hilltops over Chesapeake Bay to the rim of the Atlantic. His father owned a considerable estate, and the boy grew up among many negro servants, innumerable animals, and a regular Zoo of pets. There was a certain sense of lordship in his mind. He liked

134 Sir John Smith (c. 1531-1607) was an English soldier, diplomat and writer. He wrote this in a letter to Lord Burghley, (1520-1598) an English statesman and chief adviser to Elizabeth I, who served as Secretary of State and Lord High Treasurer. This letter, written circa 1589-1590, is about English soldiers serving in Flanders. It probably became well known at this time with World War One, which saw British troops serve in Flanders. "In truth, they were young Gentleman, Yeoman and Yeoman's Sons, and Artificers of the most brave sort, such as went voluntarily to serve of a gaiety and joyalty of mind; all which kind of people are the Flower and Force of a Kingdom."
135 F.W. Robertson was an English preacher (1816-1853). He had a nervous breakdown and went to Switzerland, and died fairly young. The phrase "troubadour of God" we could not find tied to his name, but it may well have been written of him. The phrase seems to have originated in writings about the life of Francis of Assisi.

his own way, felt himself irritated by check, stung by

correction, and incapable of seeing life from any point of view but his own.

During his boyhood the central figure of the family life was a venerable snow-capped grandmother, more Victorian than Victoria herself, mildly morbid about a long-deceased husband, evangelical, rigid concerning the proprieties, her austere and commanding face sternly set against invading vulgarity, but copious and anecdotal, with an interest in the living world, albeit an interest chiefly anxious concerning its future.

Under the shadow of this impressive relic of a vanished antiquity the soul of the mutinous boy was chilled into some semblance of reverence, coming from his ponies and dogs into her presence with the sense of entering another world, breathing a different climate, speaking an unnatural language.

It was only when he was alone with his mother that he felt stirrings within him of tenderness and graciousness. He told me that she was "always interested in what I was doing, but never solicitous"—a telling phrase good for all mothers to lodge in their hearts. His mother never gave him the feeling that he was being watched; he could talk to her without the paralysing fear that she was listening only in order to correct; a beautiful frankness, a real interest in his affairs, a quick willingness to help him on his own level, characterised her attitude; and when he wished to be alone she understood and withdrew to other occupations.

From this mother he learned to think of a transcendent Being who had created the heavens and the earth, and of His Son Jesus, who had lived among men, who had taught them how to live, and who had been cruelly put to death by wicked enemies.

This teaching was associated in his mind with the different activities which marked one day in the week, when he had to be more careful in his use of soap and flannel, when his best suit was put out for him, and when he went in company with his parents to a church carrying on the Anglican tradition. There, too, he found the secular importance of his father duly acknowledged, for his father was one of the "patrons" of that church, and was ever received with a certain deference by the other officials.

What the boy thought of God and Christ, of Heaven and Hell, of Prayers and Hymns, we do not know; for his consciousness did not become alert in such matters till he was approaching the age of fourteen. It woke suddenly to awareness, and also to enthusiasm, in rather a strange way. There came to that church one Sunday a very old clergyman who had spent long years of his life as a missionary to the mountaineers in the Far South. Such stories did he tell in his sermon, stories of pathos and heroism, stories of difficulties and endurance, stories of violent men broken down by the beauty of Christ, and bad men restored to goodness and happiness by the power of Christ, that the little boy in the big pew resolved then and there that he too would be a missionary.

The strange feature in this idea is its tenacity. It did not fly in at one door of his soul and out at the other, like Bede's sparrow;[136] it stayed there, worked there, became the master-thought of his mind. When he was in the fields, or among his animals, or talking to the negroes, this idea went to sleep; but when he came to lie down in his bed at night it awoke with a freshness that held his thoughts. He began to read the Bible with a boy's earnest attentiveness, to say his prayers with no mere formal sense of fulfilling a duty, to cultivate an interest in the history of the Church. Nevertheless, he still remained the proud and self-willed little boy of the years before this dream.

Soon after the visit of the missionary he was packed off to a

136 An anecdote from Venerable Bede's *Ecclesiastical History*: "Another of the king's chief men, approving of his words and exhortations, presently added: "The present life of man, O king, seems to me, in comparison of that time which is unknown to us, like to the swift flight of a sparrow through the room wherein you sit at supper in winter, with your commanders and ministers, and a good fire in the midst, whilst the storms of rain and snow prevail abroad; the sparrow, I say, flying in at one door, and immediately out at another, whilst he. is within, is safe from the wintry storm; but after a short space of fair weather, he immediately vanishes out of your sight, into the dark winter from which he had emerged. So this life of man appears for a short space, but of what went before, or what is to follow, we are utterly ignorant. If, therefore, this new doctrine contains something more certain, it seems justly to deserve to be followed." The other elders and king's councillors, by Divine inspiration, spoke to the same effect."

"Church School," which is an American equivalent for the English public school, and his clerical ambition was not daunted by the visible and even scandalous enmity which existed between the clergymen who taught him his lessons, preached to him in church about the gospel, and administered to him the sacrament of Holy Communion. These men hated each other quite openly, and did not hide that ugly fact, in which they gloried, from the boys under their care.

He says that the religious studies of this school were "lifeless, sapless," but gladly acknowledges that the tone was good, and says that his spiritual life was helped in the fields and by the sea. There was not a boy in the school who had come from a bad home.

From this school he proceeded to one of the best Universities of America, and soon became a figure in its most fashionable club (a form of college), ending up as a member of its Senior Council, and the President of the most distinguished Society in the University. He was of a nature to make an impression.

The war in Europe brought him in 1915 to the British Islands with a group of American University men who had volunteered to serve with the Y.M.C.A. He worked like a nigger, but confesses that if he touched one man that summer it was all he did, and that man not vitally.

His next spiritual adventure was in China, where his University maintains an important college. He says he was astonished by the wonderful machine he found in China, but more astonished by the fact that it did nothing—"machinery, but no motion." He was told by all the workers that he was doing wonderful things, but he knew very well that he was doing nothing. The business school, the gymnasium, the library, the classes, the social work— all these were crowded by young Chinamen; but what came of them? When Ruskin was told that a submarine cable had been laid between England and India he asked, "What messages will it convey?"

One day there came to this Chinese city the Surgeon of Souls, with a group of men devoted to the work of personal religion. He was pointed out to the Virginian in this fashion: "There goes a man who is doing what these missionaries and Christian workers are talking about." The Virginian took a good look at him and did not like him. He thought him crude. The attitude of the aristocratic University towards the college where F.B. had begun to work was one of supercilious contempt. The Virginian shared that contempt.

But interest in F.B. increased, and the Virginian found himself listening to stories about him. Presently he was making F.B.'s acquaintance, and found him, rather condescendingly perhaps, a person worth knowing. One day he drew F.B. aside and asked him if he would tackle a certain young Chinaman in whom he was interested. F.B. replied, "That's your job. If you haven't anything to give him by now you ought to!" The Virginian was mad. He went away, not sorrowfully, but in a towering rage.

When this temper evaporated he faced the truth of F.B.'s bitter taunt. Nothing to give! Was that really the truth? If so, how serious, how impossible, his position. He fought with himself. Was he to give up his hope of helping men? Would it always be that he had nothing to give? The question drove him to F.B.

"One day," he tells me, "we got to business. I told him, in spite of myself, my temptations and my sins. They came out almost before I knew it. For the first time they were outside myself, in words, words that startled and shamed. He understood. We got it all into the open. The position became absolutely clear. I saw at once what was keeping me from power. There was no overflow, because there was no inflow, and no inflow because sin was walling out the power of God. I tried to bring up intellectual difficulties. He refused to discuss them, would not even glance at them. This may seem to some—it didn't to me—a source of weakness; it gives the impression that he cares nothing for intellectual integrity. The truth is the man is a born mystic. Get him alone and you realise this at once. And you realise also the truth of what William James says, that we have got to accept the experience of the mystic as valid experience. F.B. made a tremendous impression on me. His simple insistence on the power of sin to wall out any vital consciousness of God was irresistible. He showed me, quite mercilessly, my spiritual impotence in the lives of other men. He laid it all bare to me, naked in broad daylight, my spiritual impotence. What good was I? Let a man ask himself that question. It's a searcher."

That night the Virginian tried to pray, but felt that his prayer was useless. He knew that he was at a turning-point. Either he would go back to America and surrender to the world, or—. The point that frightened him was this: If he took the plunge it might mean, not a decorative interest in religion, not the patronising association of a rich young man with a University scheme of social welfare, but the mission-field for life. Was he ready for that? To be a parson?

He walked about his room. "My sins," he said, "rose up before me straight as tombstones. If I took this plunge it meant a clearing up all along the line. It meant confession. It meant a break with all that had gone before—a new life. Then I saw that this was a matter of the will not of the intellect. I faced that knowledge for several moments. My will! Was I willing to do this thing, or was I not willing? A strange thought, annihilating in its effect—my little pygmy will opposed to the Will of God, my little pride sniffing at the Universe, my heart dead cold in the Presence of the Almighty! Without a scrap of emotion, but with what I can only call a great heave of my will, I knelt down to make my submission, to give myself, without reservation, to God. Usually this moment costs something in nervous energy, and results in emotional excitation. I experienced nothing of the kind. I was sensible only of calm, of a feeling that something needful and right had been done. I felt very little at the time. I simply realised that I had jumped a fence at which I had long balked. There was no breaking in of light upon me, nor anything unusual. After the prayer, which tore away a wall of my own erection—the wall of unwillingness to face God's Will fully—I prayed again, but without ecstasy. I rose from that prayer hoping that I might be used to help others, and feeling that I had done what was required of me. But I was not to be left only with that feeling. As I lay in bed there came to me a distinct Voice, and that Voice said, *There is no work of Mine to do for him who is not wholly Mine.* I cannot tell you the effect of those words. They were no words of mine. They were different from all other words I had ever heard. And they revealed to me what I believe to be the central truth of religion."

The change in the Virginian from that hour was visible to all his friends. He became the impassioned champion of personal religion. Gone for him was all hesitancy. Abandoned, too, was the attitude of a looker-on. He flung himself with a joyful enthusiasm into the work of helping men face to face, swept forward from all his former landmarks by the immediate success of his efforts. He told me that association with F.B. taught him "the absolute workability of the thing he talked about." This was no question, remember, of dogma or of ceremonial rite. It was the human question. It was a case of drowning men saved from death.[137] F.B. spoke of men who were "suffering hell," or of men lost in a fog, or of men who were missing all the things that make life splendid, and showed him those same men with shining eyes, glad voices, happy as the day is long.[138] There they were before the Virginian's eyes—miracles. Changed men! A wonderful thought; changed from darkness to light, from blindness to vision, from misery to happiness, from death to life, laughing in the joy of that change.

What a power, to do these things![139]

He exclaimed to me, "I hear people say that what men want is *something quite human.* Nonsense! What they want is something wholly and absolutely divine. The mistake lies in expressing this Divine Something in dark and mysterious language. The language must be human. But the thing itself, the mysterious Power which changes life in a moment, *that* must be shown from the first as divine. I see it in this manner: In each one of us there is a vestige of the Christ. It is the light that lighteth every man. Until sin has blotted out from consciousness the knowledge of this light, every man feels that there is something within him higher than himself. I am certain this feeling exists in all men who are not dead in sin—the greatest of men of science and the most ragged and ignorant of down-and-outers. It is there in their souls, making for a

---

137 BB, pg. 28, "We, in our turn, sought the same escape with all the desperation of drowning men."
138 BB, pg. 160, "The expression on the faces of the women, that indefinable something in the eyes of the men, the stimulating and electric atmosphere of the place, conspired to let him know that here was haven at last."
139 BB, pg. 132, "We have recovered, and have been given the power to help others."

sense of dualism, dividing their personality, distracting their unity. And I am equally convinced that when a man is acutely conscious of this division, and meditates on the best way of securing inward peace, he naturally, instinctively, inevitably turns to Christ. This is my firm conviction. It is born of experience. The surrender, if it is to be made, is to Christ, to no one else. To Christ, the lover and saviour of men. This is my theology: God has left a part of Himself in each of us, and this divine part of our nature, in every moral crisis, recognises the historic Jesus and the Christ of experience as its necessary complement. Of course, the traditional, the ecclesiastical, the theological mind has obscured Him; but I am certain that where men are unprejudiced, where they are in dead earnest about getting right, where they want unity with the whole heart, the whole spirit, and the whole mind, they turn to Christ. Let me sum it all up in a few words. What changes life is, first, a sense of sin, a haunting knowledge that the habits of sin have got one in their deadly grip, second, an experience of the *hilarity* of Christianity really lived, and, third, the immense appeal of Christ's challenge to make a new world."

On no other subject is this fighting Virginian so glad to talk as the hilarity of the religious life. "The gayest bunch of men I know," he tells you, "is the group that swings round F.B. They are fellows who have found something worth finding. We never meet but what we have a good time. This is far from the professional mirth of certain sorts of religious people. It is the laughter of men who really know there is a way out in this world, and who are doing their best to make it known to others." No defence for such happiness is necessary. It is a happiness that cannot be helped. Do men gather thorns of vines or thistles of fig-trees? As the sun shines so does the heart of a man conscious of unity with his Creator, conscious, too, of power to change human life, rejoice with a joy unknown to the victims of delusion and the slaves of sin.

In this hilarity one sees the joy of a spirit set free from the contagion of the world's slow stain, emancipated from all the petty conventions and parochial restraints of that old, unhappy world, launched definitely on the radiant ocean of eternity. The world looks upon these men as "odd," but it has no idea how odd it looks to them. What a dull world, what a sad world, what a blind world, and what a stupid, blundering world it must seem, in the eyes of men whose hearts know nothing except the bliss of conscious and unselfish union with God. The Virginian's favourite saying of Christ is the challenge, "My doctrine is not Mine, but His that sent Me. If any man will do His will, he shall know of the doctrine, whether it be of God, or whether I speak of Myself."[140] He says that those who have experienced this mighty change do not speak of what they think or of what they hope, but of what they *know*. That is the reward of a unified personality.

Even after that night when he made his submission the Virginian has grown in this knowledge. He tells me that F. B. asked him in those early days to attend a private conference on the subject of personal religion, promising him that he should meet a wonderful group of men—"All F. B.'s geese are swans; it is partly his intense enthusiasm and belief in us which keeps us functioning!" When he got to his conference the Virginian was disappointed by what looked like a lot of quite ordinary folks. The wall arose once more between him and the souls of others. F. B., reading his thoughts, drew him aside, and whispered into his ear this question, "What would you have thought of the twelve apostles?"

From that moment he learned not only to abandon a superior attitude towards others, and not only to suspect and examine the grounds of instinctive antipathy, but positively to look always for the good in others, to stand tiptoe to welcome the spiritual truth behind all physical appearances, to become a realist of human existence. The last vesture of self was torn away. He became a troubadour of God.

I profess no other share

in the selection of my lot, than this

My ready answer to the will of God

Who summons me to be His organ. All

Whose innate strength supports them shall succeed

No better than the sages.[141]

---

140 John 7:16-17.
141 "Paracelsus," a poem by Browning.

He might so easily have been a conventional figure in American life, of no more use to the universe than a mushroom, a dull, unimaginative, and self-satisfied citizen of a materialistic civilisation. Most of us say at one time or another:

The world is too much with us; late and soon,

Getting and spending, we lay waste our powers;

Little we see in Nature that is ours;[142]

but not many think how definitely dreary is such an existence, or realise that there is a way out—a way out into unity and joy.

Let any man who reads these words ask himself whether he knows any way out of this suffocating and soul-destroying materialism save only the way taken by the Virginian—that plunge away from self, that baptism in the moving waters of God—which surely we may hope are "for ever at their priest-like task of pure ablution round earth's human shores."[143] And the reward!

Are there not, Festus, are there not, dear Michal,

Two points in the adventure of the diver,

One—when, a beggar, he prepares to plunge, One—when, a prince, he rises with his pearl?

Festus, I plunge.[144]

"Again, the Kingdom of Heaven is like unto a merchant man, seeking goodly pearls, who, when he had found one pearl of great price, went and sold all that he had, and bought it."[145]

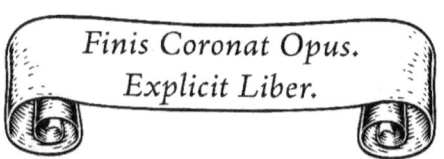

Finis Coronat Opus.
Explicit Liber.

---

142 "The World Is Too much With Us," a poem by Wordsworth.
143 Love sonnet, "Bright star, would I were stedfast as thou art," by English poet John Keats (1795-1821)
144 "Paracelsus" a poem by Robert Browning.
145 Matthew 13:45-46.

Explicit iste liber, scriptor sit crimine liber, Christus scriptorem custodiat ac det honorem

Ὥσπερ ξένοι χαίρουσιν ἰδεῖν πατρίδα, οὕτως καὶ οἱ γράφοντες ἰδεῖν βιβλίου τέλος

श्रीकृष्णार्पणमस्तु

書成矣，感盡天地

סלוע ארוב לאל חבש סלשנו סת

"of making many books there is no end; and much study is a weariness of the flesh"
- Ecclesiastes 12:12

BULKINGTON BOOKS